W9-BZF-265

A NATION WITHOUT A CONSCIENCE

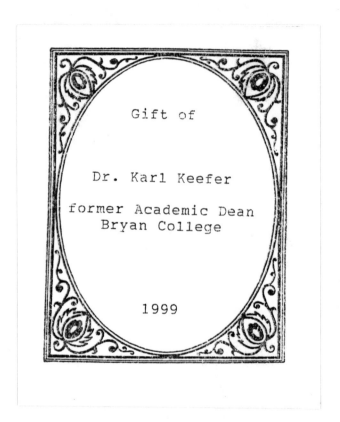

a nation without a conscience

Tim & Beverly LAHAYE

Tyndale House Publishers, Inc.
Wheaton, Illinois

Published in association with the literary agency of Alive Communications, P.O. Box 49068, Colorado Springs, CO 80949

Unless otherwise indicated, Scripture quotations are taken from the *New American Standard Bible,* © 1960, 1962, 1963, 1968, 1971, 1972, 1973, 1975, 1977 by The Lockman Foundation. Used by permission.

Scripture quotations marked NIV are taken from the *Holy Bible,* New International Version®. Copyright © 1973, 1978, 1984 by International Bible Society. Used by permission of Zondervan Publishing House. All rights reserved. The "NIV" and "New International Version" trademarks are registered in the United States Patent and Trademark Office by International Bible Society. Use of either trademark requires permission of International Bible Society.

Library of Congress Cataloging-in-Publication Data

LaHaye, Tim F.
  A nation without a conscience / Tim and Beverly LaHaye.
    p. cm.
  Includes bibliographical references.
  ISBN 0-8423-5018-7 (hard cover)
  ISBN 0-8423-8090-6 (soft cover)
    1. Christianity—United States—20th century.   2. United States—Civilization—1970.
3. United States—Moral conditions.   4. Church and social problems—United States.
I. Title.
BR526.L34   1994
277.3'0829—dc20   94-26145

Printed in the United States of America

00 99 98 97 96 95 94
8   7   6   5   4   3   2   1

Peace is normally a great good, and normally it coincides with righteousness, but it is righteousness and not peace which should bind the conscience of a nation as it should bind the conscience of an individual; and neither a nation nor an individual can surrender conscience to another's keeping.

THEODORE ROOSEVELT,
message to Congress, December 4, 1906

Conscience does not get its guidance from a Gallup poll.

ANONYMOUS

CONTENTS

INTRODUCTION

Cowardice asks, Is it safe? Expediency asks, Is it politic? Vanity asks, Is it popular? But Conscience asks, Is it right?
WILLIAM MORLEY PUNSHON[1]

Whispers. We are surrounded today by conflicting voices.

Should Americans cheat on their income tax? Only if they won't get caught, says Cowardice.

Should families spend part of the grocery money on lottery tickets? Certainly, says Expediency. The lottery supports our educational system.

Should pastors preach against homosexuality? Never! says Vanity. Such preaching isn't politically popular.

And with each question Americans ask, the quiet voice of Conscience speaks. . . .

Is anyone listening?

Conscience, someone has said, is condensed character. No one can deny that America's character has changed over the past two generations. We once depended upon the blessings of God; today we collectively mock or ignore him altogether.

Look at our laws and public policy: Our nation murders four thousand unborn babies every day; we accept the promotion of homosexuality as an "alternative lifestyle"; we license gamblers and pornographers; we excuse murderers because they are "victims." Our politicians show no shame about their pro-abortion and pro-gay positions, our children shoot each other on school playgrounds, and our tax dollars support obscenity and live bloodletting exhibitions in the name of "art."

What has happened to America's conscience?

america
without a
conscience

■ ·

1

According to [Hitler's] own words, he was without conscience.
He called conscience a Jewish invention.

WILLIAM KATZ[1]

Contrary to what Adolph Hitler claimed, there is such a thing as the conscience, a God-given innate quality that is part of what makes man different from the animals. The human conscience was evidenced in the Garden of Eden. Adam and Eve chose to eat the forbidden fruit of the tree of the knowledge of good and evil. Immediately after their disobedience, knowing then the difference between right and wrong, Adam and Eve tried to hide from God. Because of their conscience, they felt bad about what they had done.

Ever since that day, that knowledge—the conscience—has been a part of human makeup. Conscience is something with which we are born. But it can be strengthened or destroyed by the kind of childhood training a person receives from his parents, family, church, school, peers, and environment and how the person responds to choices of good and evil throughout life.

Nations, too, have a conscience. Nearly all civilizations and tribes have had laws resembling the law code given by God to Moses on Mount Sinai. In fact, Hammurabi's famous law code, which may predate the Ten Commandments, is quite similar to the Ten Commandments concerning right and wrong behavior in human interaction. This universal law code may have sprung from an unrecorded primitive revelation from God, or perhaps it sprang from the human conscience.

The apostle Paul wrote of this unique characteristic in man:

> *For when Gentiles who do not have the Law do instinctively the things of the Law, these, not having the Law, are a law to themselves, in that they show the work of the Law written in their hearts, their conscience bearing witness, and their thoughts alternately accusing or else defending them. (Rom. 2:14-15)*

Admittedly, individuals and nations do not always obey their conscience, but most feel shame when they do not.

Why? Because unless their conscience has been seared or destroyed, it will rise up and either accuse or excuse an action. This unwritten code of conduct is what our founding fathers called "natural law."

A religious nation reflects this natural conscience in its laws—it permits certain acts and forbids others. Even secular, pagan, and barbaric cultures have a system of rights and wrongs, although their choices are often arbitrary.

A nation's conscience is reflected by its public policy and the public education of its citizens. If, for example, it is illegal to steal or kill, it is only logical that children should be taught not to steal or kill. Television programming and other agents of public influence should reinforce the message that stealing and killing are wrong. Otherwise children will receive contradictory and confusing messages concerning proper moral conduct.

Have you wondered why our children's morals are confused?

HAS AMERICA LOST HER CONSCIENCE?

America is great because she is good. If America ever ceases to be good, she will cease to be great.—Alexis de Tocqueville, French historian, 1848

Has America ceased to be good? Has she lost her conscience? Consider this story:

A young black couple, married only five months, was driving on Interstate 395 in Washington, D.C., one Saturday afternoon when a carload of total strangers drew up beside them. One man in the car opened fire. The nineteen-year-old wife died instantly, and the injured husband was barely able to ease the car to a stop. When the police apprehended the killer (who would have been in prison on another charge had not a parole board cut his sentence by 60 percent in the belief that the criminal had been "rehabilitated"), the murderer gave this reason for the outrageous random shooting: "I just felt like killing someone."

The dreams of a fine young couple were shattered because a criminal without a conscience wanted to please himself.

Such actions are becoming common. In our nation's capital we now have more violent deaths each year than days of the year—more than 465 in 1993. From coast to coast our nation is witnessing an explosion of cruel and utterly conscienceless acts.

David Johnstone, a young father visiting San Francisco on business, was walking down a street when he drew the attention of three teenagers. The boys shot David in the back. The bullet severed his spinal cord, nicked his lung and kidney, perforated his colon twice, and finally lodged in his liver. He died within a month of the shooting. This angry, uncivilized action by three hostile teens left a wife widowed, and left fatherless a fourteen-year-old daughter and an eleven-year-old son.[2]

How did the San Francisco community respond to this heartless murder? It was determined that the teenage killer was himself a victim—after all, he had never met his father and had been abandoned as a baby by his drug-addicted mother. Certainly none of us would envy such a childhood, but the man was guilty of murder. But according to the San Francisco jury, the criminal was simply living according to his conditioning; he was a mere victim of circumstance.

How twisted can thinking become? Our legal system would have us consider the murderer a victim. We acquit the criminal and punish the innocent victims who often cannot speak for themselves. Taught that he is helpless and powerless to resist his impulses, a convict has no hope for change. Such thinking is based on a refusal to accept the doctrine of sin, which leaves behaviorists no alternative but to conclude that mankind is naturally good but can be corrupted by his environment and experience. Taken to its natural conclusion, behaviorism teaches that no one is ever responsible for his or her actions. People who do wrong are not to be blamed—they are just responding to what life has handed them. Is it any wonder crime is escalating?

A U.S. SENATOR SPEAKS OUT

U.S. Senator Dan Coats, a committed Christian, has publicly pointed out the need for us to "confront the moral decay of society."[3] Quoting from the authors of *Crime and Human Nature*, Senator Coats included this excerpt in an editorial published by the *Washington Times:* "No culture can survive without a moral consensus, shared beliefs about right and wrong, a common standard of truth. This is what defines the rules we live by. Without this consensus, the individual is abandoned to self-interest alone."

Senator Coats believes, with a growing multitude, that the bombarding of our 47 million school-age children with the theories of secular humanism has produced a generation of people with severely damaged consciences. On top of that, the educators who run our school system object to any mention of the Ten Commandments, any standard of moral values if they are in any way based on religion. They insist that the Constitution forbids the teaching of religion in the public schools, so any value system based on religion is also interdicted from the classroom. So our public school youth are growing up without any reinforcement except what they get at home or church.

For evidence of this moral void, Senator Coats compares the motivation for violent crimes of a generation past with those of today:

> *Crime, it was once believed, was rooted in rational acts.*
>
> *Poverty prompted robbery, burglary, or car theft. Murder had a motive—it was premeditated—or resulted from the heated passion of the moment. And other crimes were traced to discernible causes.*
>
> *But today, we are witnessing a new face of crime, a profoundly disturbing trend. Daily we read of crimes that defy any rational explanation and of perpetrators without a conscience. These examples illustrate:*
>
> *A young man named Michael Ensley was shot in his Reseda, California, high school because his assailant thought Michael gave him a "funny look."*
>
> *In Atlanta,* Newsweek *reports, a gentleman named Charles Conrad, crippled by multiple sclerosis, using a walker and a wheelchair to get around, was ruthlessly attacked and tortured by three young people all under the age of seventeen. . . . The tragic list of those affected by the new face of crime goes on and on.*[4]

6

TOTAL DISREGARD FOR HUMAN LIFE

America will tolerate the taking of human life without giving it a second thought. But don't misuse a household pet.—Dick Gregory[5]

Whenever a nation turns its back on God or begins to live as if he does not exist, it begins to show up in its citizens' disregard for human life. At one time almost every American believed in God, and that belief was reflected in the way people treated each other. Today's humanist elite, who exercise more and more control over the media, education, and, to a great extent, our government, are largely driven by humanistic values and an agenda that is neither God's nor that of the people they are supposed to serve.

The front page of the *Washington Times* on December 27, 1993, featured the picture of a seventeen-year-old boy lying in a crumpled heap, the victim of a gang shooting. The young man had been killed just minutes after he paid his respects to a friend who had been murdered two days earlier. The boy's mother and other witnesses gave the following account:

> *When me and my family first came into the funeral, he hugged all of us. He put something in the casket, a hat. He kissed him [the victim]. And he left out, crying. [sic]*
>
> *Outside the funeral home, the mourner was approached by three men, said a funeral home employee who refused to give her name. She said he ran, and the men chased him.*
>
> *The victim ran about a block to a narrow alley between red brick buildings that are part of Edison Sales, an electronics shop. He was shot several times in the alley.*[6]

Such murderers apparently have no fear of God, and unless one acknowledges that life comes from the hand of God, life really doesn't have much meaning. Nowhere in our country is that philosophy more apparent than in the legal accessibility of abortion. Every day, babies are aborted as a result of the government's policy of granting a woman the right to terminate the life of her unborn child. Each year 1.6 million such "choices" are made, totaling between 30 and 40 million such deaths since abortion was declared legal by the highest court of the land in 1973.

Is it any wonder that a nation that has legalized the slaughter of innocents in the name of "choice" and convenience is witnessing wholesale teenage slaughter? Godless humanism cheapens all life. Our current crime wave is merely the public manifestation of an empty belief system.

THE NEXT GENERATION MAY BE WORSE THAN THE PRESENT ONE

A Washington Metropolitan Police captain, deploring the increase in preadolescent slayings in recent months, said: "Earlier in the year, we had a twelve-year-old who killed his mother and stepfather because he was told they were going to have to move and that he'd have to go to another school."[7] When children would sooner kill their parents than change their residence, you know society's in trouble!

Chuck Colson, founder of Prison Fellowship, describes the problem well:

> *Twenty years ago, in the midst of Watergate, there was a battle for the government of the United States. Today, there is a*

battle for the soul of America. And that battle makes Water-gate look like child's play. Look at the headlines from recent days:

Dartmouth, Mass.: Three schoolboys stabbed a ninth-grade classmate to death, then traded high-fives and laughed.

Washington, D.C.: An unsupervised eight-year-old boy in a homeless shelter swung a twelve-week-old baby around a room, bashing his head repeatedly against the floor, "like Robocop." The baby was killed. The boy explained, "I was just playing."

This is the face of crime today—crime without reason or remorse. We are witnessing the most terrifying thing that could happen to a society: the death of conscience in a generation of young people.

The bone-chilling words of Adolf Hitler appear at the entrance of Auschwitz. Hitler wrote, "I want to raise a generation devoid of conscience." *It is an irony that the world rose up and defeated Hitler out of moral conviction, and now we in America, through our indolence and apathy, are achieving exactly what Hitler failed to do [emphasis added].*[8]

Almost every big city can tell of a mindless tragedy like that of Christine Schweiger of Milwaukee, Wisconsin. While visiting a fast-food restaurant with her ten-year-old daughter, she was accosted by two teenagers who ordered her down on her knees and then demanded her money. When Christine, an accountant and mother of three, said she didn't have any, the sixteen-year-old apparently took offense. As her daughter watched, the youth allegedly fired a twelve-gauge sawed-off shotgun at point-blank range, blasting away most of Christine's head. Police say he later explained, "I'm the big man. I got the gun. Why does she have this attitude?"

The sheriff of Milwaukee pointed out how the criminal attitude has changed. "It used to be your money or your life. Now they'll shoot you anyway."[9]

YES, VIRGINIA, WE HAVE GONE MAD!

Milwaukee school superintendent Howard Fuller made a record of the names of the teens who had been killed between January 1992 and January 1993 and observed that on the list were fifteen kids under the age of seventeen. He relates that on his visits to elementary schools to talk about education the very first question he is asked is what to do when someone starts shooting! He spends most of his time telling kids how to hide under a desk.

Have we gone mad? Yes. When innocent elementary school children are so exposed to violence that their first concern is safety from irrational gunmen, we live in a state of sheer lunacy.

Children depend upon love and protection from the adults in their world. But when we pay $500 billion in taxes to finance a secular educational system that fails to educate millions of its charges, prides itself on breaking down moral values learned at home, and permits 250,000 acts of violence in our schools *each year,* we are depriving our children of their fundamental needs.

Television violence was accused of inspiring real-life mayhem that affected 23,000 citizens in 1993, but television producers refuse to admit liability for the carnage. The power of television, with its vast potential for good and harm, is almost impossible to control under current law. The Federal Communications Commission is supposed to reform and protect the airwaves, but when it can't come up with enough legal backing to cancel the license of stations that promote promiscuity, obscenity, and violence, our nation's moral values are being affected. Television daily gives our children living examples of violent, illegal crimes that destroy human life.

On January 22, 1993, only two days after taking office, President Clinton signed an executive order lifting the ban on research using fetal tissue from elective abortions. Less than six months later, he signed the National Institute of Health Reauthorization Act, which authorized the harvesting of aborted babies for taxpayer-funded research, codifying his earlier executive order. When government will not assume the responsibility to protect even our innocent unborn, to whom can we turn? Our nation's babies are now exploited in order to prolong others' lives.[10]

VIOLENCE IS BUT ONE EVIDENCE

Although we are most likely to hear about violent deaths, rapes, and robberies on the front page of our newspaper and on our local television news program, there are many other signs of potential disaster. Teenage motherhood, continually on the rise, bears tragic consequences for these fatherless children. Millions of children growing up today will never know their father.

The National Commission on Children reports that children who live with only one parent—usually their mother— are six times more likely to be poor than children who live

11

with both parents. In addition, they are at greater risk for emotional, behavioral, and intellectual problems. Among such children there is a greater incidence of juvenile delinquency.[11] Even Senator Patrick Moynihan, a Democrat from New York, accurately noted on a news program that "the breakup of family inevitably, predictably . . . will lead to the growth of large numbers of predatory males."[12]

Since 1960, the rate of births to unmarried women has risen from 5 percent to nearly 30 percent—a nearly sixfold increase![13] This shouldn't surprise us for many no longer view sexual relations as an expression of love between a husband and wife but instead as a casual recreational activity often engaged in by virtual strangers. To some, immorality is a badge of honor rather than a matter of shame. Four of the five cheerleaders elected by one Texas high school were pregnant at the time or became pregnant soon after being chosen! A generation ago pregnant girls were so embarrassed by their condition that they would usually drop out of school or take classes by correspondence. Not so today. Many teenage mothers claim they purposely had sex so they could get pregnant—some for the welfare payments, some to prove their adulthood (as early as twelve years old), and others so they could have someone of their own to love.

Marriage has become a calculated risk. For every two marriages today, one ends in divorce. Of those who divorce, almost 90 percent remarry at least once, and a majority of those couples get a second divorce. From the numbers some might conclude that there are more unhappy marriages than happy, causing many to bypass marriage altogether, choosing instead to live together without benefit of a moral or legal commitment. Certain public policy rulings have the effect of discouraging marriage through the tax code, welfare, and no-fault divorce laws.

One of the early cases the Concerned Women for America Legal Defense Foundation took on was that of Mrs. Evelyn Smith, a Christian woman whose tenants, an unmarried couple, filed a grievance against her. Mrs. Smith had explained that her policy was to not rent to unmarried couples, so the couple gave the impression that they were married as they signed the lease. Later, when they admitted they were not married, Mrs. Smith returned their deposit and thanked them for their honesty. The matter didn't stop there. A few months later Mrs. Smith heard from the California Department of Fair Employment and Housing. The applicants had filed a grievance against Mrs. Smith on the basis of marital discrimination. In the end, judges ruled that Mrs. Smith not only needed to reverse her policy, but she also had to pay a fine for her discrimination. Sadly, this is but another example of how the law penalizes those who seek to live righteously.

The First Amendment has been so distorted that it is producing what it was written to prohibit—an established philosophy of secular humanism, which in every sense is itself an established religion—and this in a nation that once accommodated religion because its founders believed that "unalienable rights" came from God our Creator and were thus safeguarded through a relationship with him.

We hear that our rights come from a benevolent government that will decide what is right and wrong. Some in government would even make it illegal to refer to certain actions using biblical terms if doing so reflects disapproval. In other words, what the Bible refers to as sin or a "perversion" is now referred to merely as a "lifestyle" or a "sexual orientation." Anyone who insists upon using biblical terms would be guilty of a "hate crime."

THE AIDS POLICY

Our nation's handling of the AIDS crisis is one of the most blatant examples of humanistic thinking. In an effort to appear morally neutral, our nation's leaders refuse to condemn homosexuality, despite the tragic deaths to which it contributes. Most homosexual newspapers carry an obituary column reporting the names and ages of homosexuals who have died, and most deaths are a result of the AIDS virus. The average age of these who have died is in the early forties, while the national average for all men is more than seventy.

AIDS, which is still predominantly spread by male homosexual activity and the use of contaminated needles by drug users, has never been officially treated by quarantine like any other contagious disease. Under the guise of protecting the constitutional rights of homosexuals, the government seems to be granting them special privileges above and beyond those of heterosexual citizens, giving as the reason the need for government to protect minority groups under civil rights law. Instead of treating this fatal disease like any other contagious disease in society, it has been given special treatment, becoming what the director of Summit Ministries, David Noble, refers to as "the first governmentally protected disease in history."

In allowing homosexual activity to be legitimized, the

government seems to overlook the devastating consequences such behavior inflicts upon individuals engaging in it. It is not politically correct to invoke biblical teaching about homosexuality. Homosexuality advocates won't admit that perhaps the Bible's condemnation of the homosexual lifestyle was not given by God in mean-spiritedness but rather is divine instruction for the good of the individual and of humanity. As the U.S. government recommends condoms as a panacea to the promiscuous, it doesn't adequately warn its citizens that the use of such devices to prevent sexually transmitted diseases is not totally without risk because of the failure rate.

Denying the obvious, our nation spends comparatively thousands of dollars on AIDS research per patient compared to less than a dollar per patient on childhood diabetes and other killer diseases. Nearly $145,000 on the average is spent to treat each AIDS patient. Meanwhile, some public schools now present homosexuality as a legitimate "alternative lifestyle," as though each child should consider adopting it. The surgeon general of the Clinton administration, Dr. Joycelyn Elders, publicly stated that homosexuality is "wonderful," "normal," and "healthy."[14]

Our national AIDS policy gives an indication that those who control the system have no conscience. How else could they encourage a policy that would entice young, impressionable teens into such a hazardous lifestyle? The national AIDS policy also reveals the philosophy that there are no "absolute rights and wrongs." One wonders if this belief is not a reaction to someone's subconscious fear that there really might be someone "up there" who will hold people accountable for their behavior.

MOTHER EARTH

Our nation is being inundated with a flood of fables. From Vice President Al Gore to former Soviet head Mikhail Gorbachev, from country musician John Denver to cable mogul Ted Turner, our national "heroes" are falling under what author Berit Kjos calls "the spell of Mother Earth." Unfortunately, this delusional idea has become the new rage, sweeping over thousands of Americans.

In his recent book, *Earth in the Balance* (Boston: Houghton-Mifflin, 1992), the vice president attributes our global woes to bad ecology. Similarly, former Soviet president Mikhail Gorbachev offers a global return to environmentalism as a solution to modern man's woes. Cable king Ted Turner has even created the cartoon series *Captain Planet,* which combines environmentalism and pagan spiritism in an effort to promote "love" and "respect" for Planet Earth. Obviously, not everyone who is concerned about responsible behavior concerning the preservation of the environment is a "neo-pagan" or "Mother Earth" worshiper. But more and more the two seem to be associated.

Neo-paganism, the twentieth-century rendition of an ancient lie, scorns Christianity, portraying it as exploitative, abusive, and not environmentally conscious, while neo-paganism masquerades as the world's cure-all. Unfortunately, many are being deceived. Even our nation's public schools are frequently used as vehicles to promote neo-paganism. Teachers are using visualization, relaxation, concentration, and projection—the very techniques used in witchcraft—to promote neo-paganism. Christianity is

16

banned from public schools, but neo-paganism in its various forms (witchcraft, goddess worship, the occult) is allowed in some schools.

Morality does find its basis in religious faith, but not all faiths are "created equal." Some faiths demand control of all the earth. The New Age faiths, rooted in a supposed concern for Mother Earth, would subjugate all others to their own, dictating how people live, where people live, and even what they believe.

MIT: A School for Cheaters

The Massachusetts Institute of Technology, now a prestigious school of engineering, has become a school where cheating is unusually common. To be fair, numerous other campuses today are attended by students similarly devoid of conscience. After all, most of them came from our nation's liberal public schools where it is generally accepted that "there are no rights and wrongs."

Don Feder, a nationally syndicated columnist, reported that a mid-December 1993 study disclosed that "83 percent of students at Massachusetts Institute of Technology cheated at least once on a homework assignment or test during the 1991–92 school year."[15]

Feder quoted a director as spokesman from MIT concerning the cheating epidemic: "Of course it's worrisome, but we're not looking at this in a moralistic way, to say people who do this are bad and they're beyond helping." Then Feder adds, "if not 'bad,' what would you call them— honorable, trustworthy, paragons of virtue? Little wonder that such high percentages of college students are admitted

17

cheats, when our culture can't bring itself to unequivocally condemn conduct that's clearly wrong."[16]

Is it any wonder that we have notorious stockbrokers who go to jail for insider trading and stock manipulation that costs innocent people millions of dollars? Or that certain thrifts, banks, and savings and loans had to be bailed out by the government with hundreds of millions of dollars? These people were caught because their activities were illegal, and it is sobering to realize they did not consider them immoral.

Charles Colson, in his excellent book *Against the Night*, tells this instructive story:

> *During a meeting of college educators at Harvard University in the autumn of 1987, President Frank Rhodes of Cornell University addressed the issue of educational reforms, suggesting it was time for universities to pay "real and sustained attention to students' intellectual and moral well-being."*
>
> *Immediately there were gasps from the audience. One angry student stood and demanded indignantly, "Who is going to do the instructing? Whose morality are we going to follow?" The audience applauded thunderously, affirming that the heckler had settled the issue by posing an unanswerable question. President Rhodes sat down, unable or unwilling to respond.*

Then Colson added,

> *In an earlier time, the obvious answer would have been to point to 2,300 years of accumulated moral wisdom, or to a rationally defensible natural law, or to the moral law revealed by God in the Judeo-Christian Scriptures. Today, however,*

few—educators or any other leaders who shape public attitudes—have the audacity to challenge the prevailing assumption that there is no morally binding objective source of authority or truth above the individual.[17]

MORAL BARBARIANS ARE EDUCATING OUR YOUTH

In a 1988 television special on education titled *America's Kids, Why They Flunk,* Barbara Walters courageously confronted parents with news they did not want to hear. Noting that our nation's children are not getting an education, she bemoaned the plummeting test scores by students, many of whom couldn't locate the United States on a world map. A significant number of the high school students she surveyed thought the Holocaust was a Jewish holiday. Then she said something profound: "The real crisis is one of character. Today's high school seniors live in a world of misplaced values. They have no sense of discipline. No goals. They care only for themselves. In short, they are becoming a generation of undisciplined cultural barbarians."[18]

Barbara Walters is right in her conclusion that we are raising "a generation of undisciplined cultural barbarians," and we shouldn't be surprised. An old truism states: A stream never rises above its source. It is unrealistic to teach an atheistic, relativistic, evolutionary philosophy of life claiming that "man is the measure of all things" and then expect our children to graduate from high school being anything but undisciplined, greedy, self-centered individuals who have a hard time maintaining long-term relationships and who have no sense of right and wrong. No wonder they will not maintain their wedding vows or take responsibility for their children or most other actions. Raised as they are today, they have no moral compass and are often hostile to those who do.

THE REAL ENEMY

You have no doubt heard of "the religious right," those who would "impose their values" on society. Most often when the secular media refers to Concerned Women for America or any of its vast membership across the country, they tag us with the label "far right" or "religious right." What most people don't realize is that the "nonreligious left," as one might call them in response, have already imposed their antimoral values on us. In the name of freedom they have fostered a society that is safe for pornographers, blasphemers (even on the so-called federally controlled airwaves), and perverts—"abusers of themselves," the Bible calls them.

Sporting T-shirts proclaiming We Recruit, a group that calls itself the Lesbian Avengers chose Valentine's Day in 1994 to launch a campaign promoting homosexuality. Their target? Elementary school students. Their tactic? Passing out candy and leaflets with the message that "some girls will grow up to love girls."[19] In addition, they gave the children an 800 number. Look who's trying to force their values—or lack thereof—on others! Did the ACLU file a suit against the Lesbian Avengers? No. But if evangelicals were passing out tracts in front of an elementary school before class, it is a virtual certainty that the ACLU would file a suit against them.

Some have even gone so far as to seek to liberalize laws against child pornography and pedophilia. In the fall of 1993, the Clinton administration sought to seize upon *Knox v.*

United States in an effort to loosen child pornography laws. Republican Congressman Chris Smith of New Jersey aptly described the administration's role as an "unholy alliance between Clinton and the porn peddler," noting that it could "only lead to the proliferation of child pornography and the further exploitation of America's children."[20]

To the relief of the majority of Americans, Congressman Smith's views were shared by all of his senatorial colleagues, who voted unanimously to pass an amendment criticizing the Clinton administration's proposed liberalization of child pornography laws. For the moment, our laws still protect children from sexual exploiters. Organizations such as the National Law Center for Children and Families, a conservative antipornography group located in Fairfax, Virginia, are vigilant in their efforts to maintain high standards and just laws to protect children from sexual exploitation.

Jean-Jacques Rousseau, the atheistic Swiss philosopher, is still quoted often on college campuses today. Many current theories of education are based on the concepts of this eighteenth-century skeptic whose philosophy did much to degrade France. One of his basic beliefs was the "perfectibility of man." He was not the first, of course, to hold such an unfounded and flawed theory. Pythagoras, four centuries before Christ, had the same idea when he said, "Man is the measure of all things." Instead of a God-centered worldview, humanists of every age have embraced a man-centered approach to life.

History opposes the humanist, for it invariably teaches that apart from God's grace, man is a moral barbarian. Rousseau was no exception. He never married the mistress with whom he lived in Paris, even though she bore him five illegitimate sons—all of whom he abandoned in a Paris foundling home. That educated barbarian may be a respected leader of today's educational elite who have adopted his Enlightenment theories into modern secular humanist education, but he obviously lacked a moral conscience.

It takes a healthy conscience to be a man or woman of character, self-discipline, commitment, and godliness—qualities that the Bible upholds. But where God is despised, so are these values. And when this happens, society is at great risk.

Morality cannot endure where right and wrong do not exist. True right and wrong cannot exist where the true God is not acknowledged. How long can a nation survive without morality?

Otto Scott knew that a foundation of religion is necessary for the sustenance of good government and civilization:

> *In terms of human history, religion is older than governments. There is no record anywhere, at any time, of any human society without a religion. There is, similarly, no great civilization that has ever arisen without a religion—and no great civilization that has ever outlasted the loss of its religion.*[21]

Pat Buchanan, syndicated columnist, commented on the superiority of America's religious-based culture when he said,

> *When the European explorers arrived here, the Aztecs were still into human sacrifice, and the locals had not yet invented the alphabet or the wheel. To call all cultures "equal" is political correctness at the expense of truth.*

The root of any culture is the "cult" or religion. The religion of the West, and of most Americans, is Christianity. And Christians believe the Founder of their faith is the Son of God, whose teachings, true for all time, are contained in the "greatest book ever written."[22]

As George Washington accurately observed in his "Farewell Address," national morality cannot prevail apart from religious principle:

And let us with caution indulge the supposition that morality can be maintained without religion. Whatever may be conceded to the influence of refined education on minds . . . reason and experience forbid us to expect that national morality can prevail in exclusion of religious principle.[23]

Our nation's first president was not alone in his conviction of the need for God's assistance in the success of our national experiment. Even Benjamin Franklin, who is not known for his moral piety, urged his congressional colleagues to bear in mind their need of divine assistance for social prosperity. Would that the following words of his were engraved in the minds of our national policymakers:

In the beginning of the contest with Britain, when we were sensible of danger, we had daily prayers in this room for Divine protection. Our prayers, Sir, were heard, and they were graciously answered. All of us who were engaged in the struggle must have observed frequent instances of a super-

23

intending Providence in our favor. . . . And have we now forgotten this powerful Friend? Or do we imagine we no longer need His assistance?

I have lived, Sir, a long time, and the longer I live, the more convincing proofs I see of this truth: "that God governs in the affairs of man." And if a sparrow cannot fall to the ground without His notice, is it probable that an empire can rise without His aid?

We have been assured, Sir, in the Sacred Writings that except the Lord build the house, they labor in vain that build it. I firmly believe this. I also believe that, without His concurring aid, we shall succeed in this political building no better than the builders of Babel: we shall be divided by our little, partial local interest; our projects will be confounded; and we ourselves shall become a reproach and a byword down to future ages. And what is worse, mankind may hereafter, from this unfortunate instance, despair of establishing government by human wisdom and leave it to chance, war or conquest.

I therefore beg leave to move that, henceforth, prayers imploring the assistance of Heaven and its blessing on our deliberation be held in this assembly every morning before we proceed to business.[24]

Can we make a better, more harmonious world without God's assistance? Has this generation evolved morally to the point where it no longer needs the divine assistance for which Benjamin Franklin so passionately called?

Just read your morning newspaper, and you'll find the answer there. Mankind needs God. We need his moral standard. Just as you and I cannot survive long without oxygen, so morality is doomed without God.

Our major institutions today are inhabited by a generation of barbarians who, claiming to be working for freedom and justice for all, are by their efforts furthering the degradation of our society. Do our leaders in government, the media, education, and the entertainment industry realize what destruction they are wreaking? Maybe, maybe not. They are the mind-benders of this society. But regardless, the harsh reality remains: We are producing Hitler's dream—a generation devoid of conscience.

> *A society that seduces the conscience by sweet reason is one thing, but ours is developing into a society that harpoons the conscience and tows it right into the maws of the mother vessel, there to be macerated and stuffed into a faceless can.—* *William F. Buckley Jr.*[25]

our conscience quieted:

THE MOST BARBARIC CENTURY IN HISTORY

2

Contrary to its promise, the twentieth century became mankind's
most bloody and hateful century, a century of hallucinatory
politics and of monstrous killings.

ZBIGNIEW BRZEZINSKI[1]

I believe that we do face a crisis in Western culture, and that
it presents the greatest threat to civilization since the barbarians
invaded Rome. . . . The new barbarians are all around us. . . .
This time the invaders have come from within.

CHARLES W. COLSON[2]

The barbarians are not at the gates. They are inside the gates and
have academic tenure, judicial appointments, government grants,
and control of the movies, television, and other media.

DAVID A. NOEBEL[3]

Who would have believed that the word *barbarian* would one day be commonly used to describe the people of *this* century? And yet, well-known policymakers and observers from vastly different backgrounds and points of view are doing so—from former National Security Advisor Zbigniew Brzezinski to Christian educator David Noebel.

It seems that liberals and conservatives alike have come to realize that this nation is now reaping the dividends of more than seventy-five years of a prevalently secularist philosophy. This philosophy, which has become the prevailing philosophy of our schools, government, entertainment industry, and media, has transformed this nation from a free society in which individuals were responsible for their own behavior to a nation that depends increasingly on a powerful and ever-growing government to solve man's problems and provide for his welfare. In the last seventy-five years we have watched young people grow into self-indulgent hedonists who have no time for God or his moral values. They demand instant gratification without sacrifice and expect government to protect them from the results of their high-risk behavior.

Consider the modern demand to be sexually promiscuous without reaping the consequences of such immoral behavior. An increasing number of our citizens believe that it is the government's responsibility to provide subsidized abortions, medical treatment for sexually transmitted diseases, contraceptives, and child care should the mother "choose" to carry her baby to term. In addition, these folks are asking the government to spend billions of dollars on research for the cure of illnesses with little evidence of trying to curtail the acts that cause the diseases. Widespread licentiousness has spawned the emergence of sexually transmitted diseases unknown just a generation ago. One of these, the AIDS virus, has reached almost epidemic proportions in just one decade. AIDS has already claimed more than 500,000 victims, and more than 3.5 million people have contracted HIV, the virus that leads to AIDS.

It has become "politically incorrect" to accuse male homosexuality of being the major reason for the spread of the disease, and those who do speak out against it may be accused of "hate crimes."

TWENTIETH-CENTURY POLITICALLY PROMPTED WARS

Zbigniew Brzezinski, national security advisor to President Jimmy Carter, illustrates in his book *Out of Control* what happens when mankind rejects God and his laws. He points out that after World War I "the ruling elite" put their confidence in man's ability to solve man's moral problems through government. Growing faith in the scientific revolution generated optimism about mankind's future condition, and the onset of the twentieth century was hailed as the real beginning of the Age of Reason:

> *And reason expressed through science, indeed, did help to transform the world for the better. The twentieth century experienced unprecedented scientific breakthroughs. . . . But this progress, unfortunately, was not matched on the moral level—with politics representing the twentieth century's greatest failure [emphasis added].*
>
> *Contrary to its promise, the twentieth century became*

mankind's most bloody and hateful century, a century of hallucinatory politics and of monstrous killings. Cruelty was institutionalized to an unprecedented degree, lethality was organized on a mass production basis. The contrast between the scientific potential for good and the political evil that was actually unleashed is shocking. Never before in history was killing so globally pervasive, never before did it consume so many lives, never before was human annihilation pursued with such concentration or sustained effort on behalf of such arrogantly irrational goals.[4]

Brzezinski's claims are not exaggerated. Indeed, it is estimated that Hitler's Third Reich caused the deaths of 17 million people—among them Jews, Gypsies, Poles, and prisoners of war. Stalin's reign of terror resulted in even more deaths. Historians say that anywhere from 20 to 25 million people died in labor camps, through artificial famines, and in outright executions. Mao's imposition of communism on China resulted in the deaths of 29 million Chinese—among them landlords, wealthy bourgeois, and peasants who didn't take well to forcible collectivization! How ironic that throughout their tragic reign, Hitler, Stalin, and Mao claimed to be working to improve the lot of the average citizen by producing a "better society."

Twentieth-Century Deaths by War

Of those who did not die as a result of the impact of totalitarian regimes, record numbers were killed in the many wars of this century.

During the twentieth century, no less than one hundred sixty-seven million lives—and quite probably in excess of one hundred seventy-five million—were deliberately extinguished through politically motivated carnage. That is the approximate equivalent of the total population of France, Italy, and Great Britain; or over two-thirds of the total current population of the United States. This is more than the total killed in all previous wars, civil conflicts, and religious persecutions throughout human history. *These horrendous though dry numbers are also a reminder of what can happen when humanity's innate capacity for aggression becomes harnessed by dogmatic self-righteousness and is enhanced by increasingly potent technologies of destruction [emphasis added].*

The above estimates of total deaths cannot convey—and, given their scale, the human mind cannot even comprehend—the cumulative damage and the moral degradation inherent in the twin cataclysms of the twentieth century: its massive wars and its totalitarian revolutions.[5]

If any should still doubt that the twentieth has been the most barbaric century in the history of mankind, Brzezinski concludes:

From a cultural point of view, both Nazism and communism represented nothing less than the modern variants of barbarism. In both instances, the totalitarian revolutions inflicted— and did so deliberately—irreparable and immeasurable damage to mankind's cultural heritage. In this respect, the Nazis acted in Germany and in occupied Europe in a manner basically indistinguishable from the frenzied efforts of the Communists in Russia or China to wipe out the cultural attainments of the preceding generations. It is impossible to account for the churches or temples blown up, for the monuments torn down, for the library collections robbed or burned, for the artworks stolen, for other cultural heirlooms plundered or destroyed. . . . But all that pales in comparison to the cumulative toll of about one hundred seventy million human beings destroyed by wars and totalitarian genocide. This estimate provides perhaps the only quantifiable dimension of the political insanity that mankind experienced during this century.[6]

But the "political insanity" to which Brzezinski refers is not the only illness plaguing the modern world. In fact, it is merely a symptom of a deeper root cause.

The Death of Human Life

All who live must die. It's an indisputable fact that we couldn't change if we tried. God has said in his Word: "It is appointed for men to die once and after this comes judgment" (Heb. 9:27). While death is an inevitable reality, it is not to be our passion or obsession. Nevertheless, for many today, it very sadly is.

The following paragraph is taken from a review of the new book *Come As You Are: The Story of Nirvana.* Nirvana is a rock group that spawned the new category of "grunge rock," and its leader was Kurt Cobain:

With its chronicle of Cobain's struggles to overcome heroin addiction . . . the book seemed destined to stand as an

32

obituary last month when the singer overdosed on champagne
and prescribed tranquilizers, then sank into a coma. Prepar-
ing to resume an interrupted European tour, Cobain is
recovered now, his rather bent sense of humor, fans would
hope, intact. He had wanted, Cobain told [the book's author]
to title In Utero, *Nirvana's last album,* I Hate Myself and I
Want to Die. *"That's what our songs are about," he said. "So*
I thought it was appropriate." [7]

Before the magazine containing this book review even hit
newsstands, it became apparent to the world that Cobain's
preferred title wasn't a joke at all. The twenty-seven-year-old
singer bought a shotgun and shot himself.

Contemporary music idolizes death. Groups choose
names like The Grateful Dead, Megadeath, and Guns and
Roses, to name a few. Our entertainment only reflects the
deeper reality of our era. Television and movies are replete
with violence and destruction. The late great American
novelist Walker Percy considered this century the most
savage, inhuman, and murderous mankind has ever
known, labeling it "the century of death."[8] Zbigniew
Brzezinski went so far as to call it the "Century of Megadeath," writing,

This century's wars extinguished no less than approximately
87 million lives, with the numbers of wounded, maimed, or
otherwise afflicted being beyond estimate. These staggering
numbers are matched and morally even overshadowed by a
still more horrifying total, one that justifiably stamps the
twentieth century as the century of megadeath: the number

33

of defenseless individuals deliberately put to death because of doctrinal hatred and passions.[9]

Night after night we hear about the slaughter of more victims in Bosnia, South Africa (before their elections in May 1994), and other parts of the world. Senseless slaughter has become so routine that we scarcely feel the pain unless it strikes someone we know. Still, we are shocked by the cruel carnage when people are murdered as they walk to the market on a Saturday morning or ride a city subway. We are horrified to think that violent death may lurk just down the street.

As shocked and horrified as Americans are at such news, we seem to have forgotten that another kind of destructive and gratuitous slaughter is occurring, *legally*, in our own cities and towns. This second slaughter involves what Dr. Bernard Nathanson has called "the silent scream," so named after the gaping mouth of a writhing fetus during an abortion. Have we forgotten our unborn?

Why have we allowed our national conscience to be quieted as innocent children are being destroyed by their mothers and doctors before their eyes have seen the light of day? In defiance of logic and instinct, we abort our babies, and yet we are shocked to find murderers in our midst. How can we teach relativism and expect our children to be morally upright?

The proabortion Alan Guttmacher Institute, the research arm of Planned Parenthood, reports that anywhere from 36 to 53 million abortions were performed worldwide in 1987 alone.[10] We condemn Hitler, Stalin, and Mao for the atrocities their regimes committed toward their fellowman, but are our "civilized" leaders any better than they? In terms of numbers, we cruelly extinguish more lives annually than any of them did in their entire regime! When it comes to abortion, the holocaust may be hidden and the scream may be silent, but there is one who sees and hears. To him will we all one day give an account.

Mother Teresa of Calcutta had a unique opportunity to speak out on behalf of the unborn at the National Prayer Breakfast held in Washington, D.C., on February 3, 1994. Many distinguished guests were present, including the president of the United States and his wife. Mother Teresa began by making her case for the ultimate need for love in the world, mentioning God the Son, who gave his life for us: "Love, to be true, has to hurt. I must be willing to give whatever it takes not to harm other people and, in fact, to do good to them. . . . It hurt Jesus to love us."

Speaking of the poor, the hungry, the thirsty, the homeless, and the abandoned, she urged her audience to follow in Jesus' footsteps by loving others. She explained that to "neglect to love brings spiritual poverty." With those words as a backdrop, Mother Teresa then went to the heart of the matter:

> *But I feel that the greatest destroyer of peace today is abortion, because it is a war against the child, a direct killing of the innocent child, murder by the mother herself. And if we accept that a mother can kill even her own child, how can we tell other people not to kill one another.* . . . Any country that accepts abortion is not teaching its people to love, but to use any violence to get what they want. *This is why the greatest destroyer of love and peace is abortion.*
>
> *Many people are very, very concerned with the children of*

35

India, with the children of Africa where quite a few die of hunger, and so on. Many people are also concerned about all the violence in this great country of the United States. These concerns are very good. But often these same people are not concerned with the millions who are being killed by the deliberate decision of their own mothers. And this is what is the greatest destroyer of peace today—abortion which brings people to such blindness *[emphasis added]*.

Mother Teresa closed her address with these words of hope and exhortation:

If we remember that God loves us, and that we can love others as he loves us, then America can become a sign of peace for the world. From here, a sign of care for the weakest of the weak—the unborn child—must go out to the world. If you become a burning light of justice and peace in the world, then really you will be true to what the founders of this country stood for.

Amen. Once we were a nation that offered refuge and opportunity to the pilgrims of the world who were eager to discover new horizons and seek true freedom. Today we are on a par with the murderous regimes of the century because of our abortion record: more than 30 million killed over the last twenty years in the United States following the dreadful Supreme Court decision in *Roe v. Wade.*

Speaking on behalf of the unborn child in the U.S. House of Representatives in June 1993, Congressman Henry Hyde made a persuasive case against abortion:

Now, my colleagues, the French have a marvelous gift for phrasemaking, and one of their marvelous phrases is: cri de coeur, a cry of the heart, and there are two cries of the heart in every human being's life. The very first cry of the heart occurs in the womb, and if my colleagues have ever looked at a sonogram picture of a little baby in the womb, they would know that is when the first cri de coeur occurs: I want to be born. It is a reflection of instincts, the urge to survive. It is inaudible, but it is there: I want to be born.

And the second cry of the heart is at the end of our lives. It is the last thing we say: I don't want to die, I don't want to die.

Mr. Chairman, I would suggest to my colleagues that abortion violates both of those cries. It violates one's right to be born, one's right to life, which our Declaration says is a fundamental endowment, and it is unalienable, the right to life. Abortion says no to that first cry of the heart, and at the same instance it says, "No, death will be visited upon you because you are unwanted by some people now, and so you die, you die," and so both of those cries of the heart are violated by destroying the unborn in the womb.

And I say to my colleagues, Not only do you kill the unborn when you do that, but you kill generations of progeny. You foreclose the future whenever you commit an abortion. An abortion forecloses the future for generations and generations.[11]

In addition to killing the aborted children themselves, we are annihilating any descendants they might have had. Further, in savagely killing others, we are, perhaps unknowingly, destroying a fundamental part of ourselves—our conscience.

Congressman Hyde, recognizing this, attempted to resuscitate what remained of his colleagues' battered ethics:

> *Think for a moment. I say to my colleagues, If you can, exercise your moral imagination, and think about the other party to the abortion decision, the unborn being, the child who might write the book, the child who might compose the symphony, the child who might discover the cure, the child who might lead his country in a time of peril. That child has no one to hear, I want to be born. Answer that cry of the heart with your vote today.*

Today one in three Americans is aborted. One-third of our population is decimated by their mothers. Even the animal kingdom is not that barbaric. Most mothering animals fight and would kill the enemy who would destroy their young. As Walker Percy has observed:

> *No other time has been more life-affirming in its pronouncements, self-fulfilling, creative, autonomous, and so on—and more death-dealing in its actions. It is the century of the love of death. . . . Americans are the nicest, most generous, and sentimental people on earth . . . yet [they] have killed more unborn children than any nation in history.[12]*

The Bible asks rhetorically, "'Can a woman forget her nursing child, and have no compassion on the son of her womb?'" (Isa. 49:15). The implied answer is, "Of course not." Today, however, our national conscience has descended to such depths that many women have tried to forget their children by simply removing the "problem." But even if mothers callously cancel their offsprings' appointment with life, God has not forgotten the children.

The pastor of an evangelical church in northern Virginia gave a sermon on abortion the Sunday before the March for Life in early 1994. Seated in the pews were a mother and her eight-year-old son. "Mom, what's abortion?" he whispered during the sermon.

As clearly as she could, the mother explained abortion in terms she thought the child would understand. "Does it hurt the baby?" he asked.

"Yes, we think it does," she answered.

"Then why would anyone do that?" he asked. At the conclusion of his sermon, the pastor invited members to meet at the church before the march. The eight-year-old boy nudged his mother and said, "Mom, let's you and I go!"

Little children who haven't yet been "wised up" by years of compromise and corruption have little difficulty discerning truth and justice. They recognize that it is not the will of their heavenly Father that even "one of these little ones perish" (Matt. 18:14).

In our relationship with God, we should have the simplicity and truth of a little child. But in our generation, simplicity is replaced by intrigue and truth by deception. And how wise we think we are! When we presume to think we can outsmart our Creator and defeat him in the war of wills, we set ourselves up for a crushing and inevitable defeat.

"Truly I say to you," Jesus told his disciples, "unless you are converted and become like children, you shall not enter the kingdom of heaven" (Matt. 18:3).

THE DEMISE OF ANOTHER CIVILIZATION

No culture endures forever: Of those that have vanished . . . most have expired in consequence of internal decay.—Russell Kirk[13]

History tells us that every great civilization has flourished, then fallen. Regardless of the monuments and safeguards erected to a nation's glory, all have been destroyed. The Egyptian pyramids lie in ruins, millennia after the formidable civilization that commanded their construction. The Roman arches, which tell of their rulers' exploits and victories, remain today only as testimony of a once-outstanding civilization, long since fallen.

As is man, so is his civilization.

All flesh is grass, and all its loveliness is like the flower of the field. The grass withers, the flower fades, when the breath of the Lord blows upon it; surely the people are grass. The grass withers, the flower fades, but the word of our God stands forever. (Isa. 40:6-8)

As is man, so is the civilization he constructs. All flesh—mankind and what he makes—is as ephemeral as grass. Its glories, its beauty, its exploits all fade away, like the loveliness of the flower of the field.

If you have ever picked wildflowers growing in a field, you must have noticed how short-lived most of them are. Within a few brief hours they have wilted. God's Word tells us that even though we often entertain thoughts of personal immortality, we are as short-lived as flowers. (We think death is

40

something that happens to *other* people, not to *us*.) The Bible also talks about the vanity and deception of such thinking:

> *Their inner thought is, that their houses are forever, and their dwelling places to all generations; they have called their lands after their own names. But man in his pomp will not endure; he is like the beasts that perish. (Ps. 49:11-12)*

THE COLLAPSE OF ROME

In his book *How Should We Then Live,* the late Francis Schaeffer related historian Edward Gibbon's observations on the state of the Roman Empire prior to its demise. The characteristics he lists are strikingly similar to those of contemporary life in America:

> *Five attributes marked Rome at its end: first, a mounting love of show and luxury (that is, affluence); second, a widening gap between the very rich and the very poor (this could be among countries in the family of nations as well as in a single nation); third, an obsession with sex; fourth, freakishness in the arts, masquerading as originality, and enthusiasms pretending to be creativity; fifth, an increased desire to live off the state.*[14]

This should sound strangely familiar and could be said about America as we enter the twenty-first century.

G. Gordon Liddy, in his January 1994 *Liddy Letter,* shared a statement from Representative Newt Gingrich of Georgia. Gingrich summed up America's condition at a news conference where he promoted a bill that would require welfare recipients to work for benefits after two years (not a bad idea!):

> *You can't maintain a civilization with twelve-year-olds having babies and fifteen-year-olds killing each other and seventeen-year-olds dying of AIDS and eighteen-year-olds getting diplomas they can't read. The welfare state has just plain failed and it's failed because it reduces human beings from citizens to clients, because it . . . subjects them to rules . . . that are anti-family, anti-work, anti-property, and anti-opportunity. The challenge of our generation is to replace the welfare state.*

MATERIALISM

Francis Schaeffer pointed out that Americans seek personal peace and affluence above all else. Given those two conditions, we are content. Because our nation has enjoyed a century without war in our own land, the quality we see most dramatically emphasized in American living is affluence—prosperity, wealth, abundance.

> *As the more Christian-dominated consensus weakened, the majority of people adopted two impoverished values: personal peace and affluence.*
>
> *Personal peace means just to be let alone, not to be troubled by the troubles of other people, whether across the world or across the city—to live one's life with minimal possibilities of being personally disturbed. Personal peace means wanting to have my personal life pattern undisturbed in my lifetime, regardless of what the result will be in the lifetimes of my*

*children and grandchildren. Affluence means an overwhelm-
ing and ever-increasing prosperity—a life made up of things,
things, and more things—a success judged by an ever-higher
level of material abundance.*

Some of us pursue the false gods of personal peace and
affluence with such zeal that we're willing to kill for them.
The stories of murder committed just because the murderer wanted someone else's jacket or designer shoes have
become increasingly common in certain levels of society.
As the Bible warns us, "The love of money is a root of all
sorts of evil, and some by longing for it [and what it buys]
have wandered away from the faith, and pierced themselves with many a pang" (1 Tim. 6:10).

OBSESSION WITH SEX

*By calling our new sexual laxity a revolution, instead of, say,
a moral breakdown, we've given it a progressive halo. We've
treated the promiscuous as pioneers of love. We've learned to
call the promiscuous "sexually active," obscenity "openness,"
and abortion "choice." And we've elevated people to celebrity
for doing things that would once have made them outcasts.[15]*

Ronald Price, a Maryland teacher, was recently sentenced
to twenty-six years in prison for sexually abusing female
students. Did he cringe at the public's discovery of his hidden
sin? No. On the contrary, within months he had signed an
option to tell his story to the world through a Hollywood
movie producer! In the case of Ronald Price we can see how
far our national obsession with sex has gone. The office of

teacher, a once-trusted profession, has been scandalized and turned to fodder for the entertainment industry's addiction to crime and sex.

One would have to be blind and deaf (some may prefer "visually and audibly impaired") not to notice that virtually all advertisements use sex to sell. Whether the product is toothpaste, jeans, alcohol, or cars, sex is used to grab the viewer's attention or to subliminally imply that the product will lead to greater satisfaction in life. We have become a sex-crazed society. Promiscuity, adultery, abortion, sexually transmitted diseases, AIDS, and the government's condom ads all testify to our nation's fixation.

Morality in Media reports that "according to the Center for Population Options, a typical teenager, watching TV, will have seen nearly 14,000 sexual encounters in one year."[16] Add to that the fact that many of our nation's schools distribute condoms to students without parental consent and you can understand why teenage pregnancies are consistently on the rise.

A recent parade of homosexuals in San Francisco displayed open acts of sodomy. Those of us whose sensibilities have not yet been entirely eradicated were shocked. What was the purpose of the parade? Ostensibly to flout moral standards and help heterosexuals "get used to" perverse and immoral behavior. The more we see and hear homosexuals brazenly display their abnormal and immoral actions, the more apt we are to grow immune to the sin and have our own consciences seared.

Unfortunately, the homosexual movement doesn't stop at parades. The New York City Department of Education now sponsors indoctrination by the Gay Men's Health Crisis, which dispenses homosexual propaganda to the city's youth under the guise of presenting health information. We will spare you the details, but the practices they advocate are nothing short of revolting. Can anyone doubt that we live in a sex-crazed society? If our nation continues on its present course, Sodom and Gomorrah will look like a church picnic by comparison.

R. C. Sproul notes in his book *Lifeviews: Understanding the Ideas That Shape Society Today:*

> *At root, hedonism is a philosophy of despair. It reflects a deep-seated sense of hopelessness of people trapped on this side of the wall. It is a quasi-logical conclusion to secularism. If my life is bound by the poles of birth and death, if my life has no eternal significance, then why not grab whatever pleasure I can squeeze out of my brief time on earth?[17]*

FREAKISHNESS IN THE ARTS

> *Ron Athey is an HIV-positive performance artist who pierces himself with needles. He also carves designs into an assistant's flesh and hangs paper towels blotted with the man's blood above the audience. His performance last month, sponsored by Minneapolis's Walker Art Center, has sparked the first controversy for National Endowment for the Arts chairman Jane Alexander. One audience member fainted. Another complained: "I was surprised they could perform this and put people in danger," said Jim Berenson, who called health officials and is considering legal action. The health department said the Walker, which used about $100 of NEA funds*

for the show, took proper precautions. . . . Said Alexander, "I
appreciate some people would find this difficult. Not all art
is for everybody."[18]

We may disagree on the definition of art or the content of
good art, but we can probably agree that art is often a
reflection of a vision of life. As the director of the National
Museum of Art observed, "The art world is mirroring a
change in the social fabric, and we can't expect our cultural
expression to be unified when the culture itself is going
through such wrenching change."[19]

Jane Alexander, the chairman of the National Endowment
for the Arts under the Clinton administration, stated essen-
tially the same thing: "Art is the expression of one's perception
of life, made manifest through imagination, intellect, emo-
tion, and what we call the soul."[20] If Miss Alexander is right
in saying that art is the expression of one's view, what does
modern art tell us about our generation?

Look at the works of "art" that ignited the controversy at the
National Endowment. Almost all were desecrations of Chris-
tian images. Andreas Serrano submerged a crucifix in a vat
of his own urine. Robert Mapplethorpe took a statue of the
Virgin Mother of God and twisted it into a bloody tie rack.

Writing in an art catalog funded by NEA, an AIDS
activist called Cardinal John O'Connor a "fat cannibal from
that house of walking swastikas up on Fifth Avenue." That
"house of walking swastikas" was St. Patrick's Cathedral,
subsequently desecrated by militants who spat consecrated
hosts on the floor at Sunday Mass.[21]

46

In a rare public appearance, the eminent Aleksandr Solzhenitsyn recently expressed his concerns over the belligerence and misdirection of art in the twentieth century. Speaking before an audience at the National Arts Club in New York City, he observed that art has been "repeatedly upset by a falsely understood 'avant-gardism'—a raucous, impatient 'avant-gardism' at any cost."[22]

It seems that twentieth-century art, while congratulating itself on its "freedom" and "creativity," is, in reality, "an empty pursuit of novel forms . . . [which lowers] the standards of craftsmanship . . . to the point of slovenliness and artistic crudity, at times combined with a meaning so obscured as to shade into unintelligibility."[23]

Art, Solzhenitsyn asserts, is an accurate indicator of what is to come. The aggressive impulse in Russia and its manifestations—art—"foretold the most *physically* destructive revolution of the 20th century [the Communist takeover of Russia],"[24] he observes.

Is art the cause or simply a reflection of our national malaise? Solzhenitsyn believes the latter, for a century of spiritual illness could yield nothing but pervasive illness in art. If man departs from God, chaos is inevitable.

Looking intently, we can see that behind these ubiquitous and seemingly innocent experiments rejecting "antiquate" tradition there lies a deep-seated hostility toward any spirituality. This relentless cult of novelty, with its assertion that art need not be good or pure, just so long as it is new, newer, and newer still, conceals an unyielding and long-sustained attempt to undermine, ridicule, and up-

root all moral precepts. There is no God, there is no truth, the universe is chaotic, all is relative.[25]

A godless, hedonistic society will inevitably manifest a hatred of God and his precepts.

Desire to Live Off the State

Robert Nisbet, a former professor of sociology at Columbia University, has noted that in the Roman Empire excessive government intrusion destroyed the republic and enslaved the family to state compliance.

> *The history of Rome, from Republic to Empire, [was] among other things, a death struggle between the family, powerful in the Republic, and the state or public power that destroyed the Republic and in the process put the family in permanent bondage to the state. The law of corporations, as the Roman lawyers called it, involved the absorption by the imperial state of virtually all associations, however traditional or voluntary.*[26]

More than ever before in our nation's history, we are seeing an ever-enlarging government that has stepped in to provide for our education, welfare, retirement, mail, and now, even our health care. In days past, the church and strong social structures of communities did much to meet the needs of those in their vicinity. Today, however, having replaced a love of God with love of pleasure, we are substituting commitment to our fellowman with taxes to our government—relegating to government the duty of caring for our fellowman.

Is government really the solution to our personal and national woes? Does more government help a problem or exacerbate it? President Abraham Lincoln had this to say on the subject: "You cannot help men permanently by doing for them what they could and should do for themselves." Excessive government fosters dependence—not independence.

Certainly we see today that the lofty goals of Roosevelt's "New Deal," Johnson's "Great Society," and other similar government initiatives led directly to the undermining of the people and institutions they were intended to bolster. Welfare, while perhaps initially helping some, ultimately destroyed initiative, drive, and industry among the indigent. And our government, despite its litany of failures, increasingly insists upon playing "almighty Provider," while simultaneously discouraging social involvement on the part of religious organizations.

Has our nation's citizenry always been so fixated on government handouts and multilevel interference? Not at all. The words of a Democratic senator in the 1930s speak to this:

> I wish Patrick Henry were living today. I wonder what he would think of the whims and vagaries in government.
>
> If Patrick Henry were living, he would not cure one evil with a multitude of other evils. When the Democratic party in convention assembled declared against a high tariff and promised to abolish or modify it, it did not mean that it would institute another system that would rob 56,000,000 people out of both pockets at the same time. . . .
>
> If Patrick Henry were living, could he be bamboozled by

talk of federal aid to the States? . . . When the government
needs money it goes down into your pocket and gets it.[27]

There is growing and legitimate concern today that the
government in the United States is stepping over the constitutional bounds that were established to limit its role in
society. In addition to the fact that government intrusion is
taking more and more taxes, we ought to be concerned about
our individual rights. We are learning through experience that
individual rights decrease in direct proportion to increases in
government interference.

Putting themselves in the place of God, government authorities are more and more often determining which beliefs
and practices are permissible and which are not. Society is
being conditioned to look to government, not God, for
guidance. There is an attitude that "Big Brother" will take care
of us. As columnist Joseph Sobran puts it, there is a trend for
people to see their "rights," not as coming from the Creator,
but rather as being founded upon state sufferance and, therefore, dependent upon the whims of the state.

> *We are less and less certain what we are still allowed to do.*
> *This is quite a reversal. Our old philosophy held that our*
> *rights are from God, and that the state merely acknowledges*
> *and respects them.*[28]

Who benefits when government grows beyond its legitimate bounds? Thomas Sowell, economist and senior fellow at the Hoover Institution, says, "The only clear
beneficiaries of activist government policies are the people

in government, whose egos are allowed full play, to use the rest of the people as guinea pigs for their bright ideas and social experiments."[29]

William Buckley Jr. is equally forthright in his opposition to activist government: "Enthusiasts for government will list the benefits of government: free schooling, health care, the lot," writes Buckley. "Well, the slavemasters also provided food, lodging, and medical care."[30]

GOVERNMENT OVER GOD

Like a virus multiplying in its host, expansive government is controlling domains over which it has no legitimate authority. One such domain is that of religious faith and expression.

In Washington, D.C., John Wimberly Jr., the pastor of Western Presbyterian Church, has been told his church can no longer carry out its ministry of feeding the hungry—this despite the recent passage of the Religious Freedoms Restoration Act! In an editorial letter to *The Washington Post*, Pastor Wimberly puzzles over the government muzzle applied on many in the religious community:

> *What is it then that moves government officials, at this critical moment when there are so many pressing needs before us, to put a muzzle on the voice of religious dissent in their midst, to put zoning locks on the doors of religious buildings that prohibit religious folks from using our buildings in ways consistent with our faith? I simply don't know.*
>
> *What I do know is that if those who are trying to restrict, control, dominate and intimidate the religious community are successful, our society will collapse under the weight of*

monochromatic thinking. We will die from an abnormal homogeneity.[31]

What more can we say? We are witnessing in America the demise of a once-great culture and civilization founded upon an acknowledgment and reverence of God. Built upon much of the heritage of Anglo law—which, as the preeminent conservative Russell Kirk observes, "accomplishes the impossible reconciliation of liberty and order"—America's foundation is being systematically undermined and demolished. What is intended to replace it? A faulty and fallacious "new politics of meaning" embraced by a very select and secretive political elite interested in furthering their vision of social utopia.

Our nation's problem is not that we have lost our political moorings—that is a mere symptom of a systemic malaise. Rather, we have lost our national conscience founded upon a reverence for God. The fruits of our departure are the love of entertainment and indulgence, an obsession with sex, bizarre art, and an ever-burgeoning state.

The current generation knows little about significance, but much about "safe sex." What will our coming generation be like given the dramatic decline we've experienced in a few short years? One young observer makes this pitiful forecast:

Anyone with an interest in the future of American society— need only to turn on MTV, watch "Beavis and Butt-Head" and understand what the next century will be like.

The founding principle will be nihilism. Rampant disregard for other living things (e.g., hitting frogs with a baseball bat) will be in. Taking responsibility for one's actions will be out.[32]

We are afraid that short of God's great mercy and our imminent repentance, America will surely go the way of the nations, leaving behind shattered lives and decrepit monuments of our failed dreams.

THE ROOT CAUSE OF COLLAPSE: MEN HAVE FORGOTTEN GOD

In the introduction to *The Assault on Religion: Commentaries on the Decline of Religious Liberty* (Lanham, Md.: University Press of America, 1986), Russell Kirk cites an address given by Aleksandr Solzhenitsyn in which the Russian writer and social observer capsulizes a truth many of us know intuitively. It is one he had heard given by older people as an explanation for the disasters that had befallen Russia: "Men have forgotten God; that's why all this has happened." Solzhenitsyn himself came to fully embrace this conclusion.

> *If I were called upon to identify briefly the principal trait of the entire twentieth century . . . I would be unable to find anything more precise and pithy than to repeat once again: "Men have forgotten God."* The failings of human consciousness, deprived of its divine dimension, have been a determining factor in all the major crimes of our present century *[emphasis added]*.

WHAT WE CAN DO

Is man basically good? Is he morally neutral? Or is he what the Bible declares him to be—created in God's image but fallen and in need of redemption? If ever there was a time in history in which man's nature was clearly manifested, that

53

time is the twentieth century. Those living in this century have witnessed war upon war, brutal leader after brutal leader, crime upon crime, even disease upon disease.

Determined to improve matters without the touch of the Master's hand, we are like the beggar who lost his wallet in Times Square but went to another part of the city to find it because the lighting was better there. We foolishly refuse to recognize the truth that unless we return with all of our heart to the Lord Jesus Christ, we will never recover the moral ground we have lost as a nation, and worse, we will have some weighty accounting to do on the Day of Judgment.

What we can do as individuals may seem limited. But each of us must assume responsibility for the part we play in building up or tearing down society by the way we live, the way we speak out or stay silent, and the way we try to be "salt and light" wherever we are. Colson expressed it well:

> *The barbarians are coming. The Lord Jesus Christ is coming. Let the church that is here come now with Good News, with the only durable Good News, and come in time.—Charles Colson*[33]

A similar statement was made at the 1994 National Religious Broadcasters' Convention during an introduction of Charles Colson, "The barbarians are coming. The Lord Jesus Christ is coming, and the Church doesn't know if it's coming or going."

our
conscience
formed:

3

We have no government armed with power capable of contending
with human passions unbridled by morality and religion.
Avarice, ambition, revenge or gallantry would break the strongest
cords of our Constitution as a shale goes through a net.
Our Constitution was made only for a moral and religious people.
It is wholly inadequate to the government of any other.

JOHN ADAMS[1]

A good conscience is a continual Christmas.

BENJAMIN FRANKLIN[2]

Why has America prospered and become the world's leading nation? One reason is that our country was founded by religious people. Even as the Pilgrims settled at Plymouth Rock in 1620, their motivation for braving the

55

hardships of this untamed new world was their desire for religious freedom and the opportunity to raise their children in their faith.

The monarchical governments of Europe at that time gave little place for freedom of religion or individual freedom in general. People were considered wards of the state and adherents to the state church, which they supported by their taxes, willingly or unwillingly. In France and Italy the Catholic Church dominated the government; in England, people supported the Anglican Church. In Germany and the Scandinavian countries, the Lutheran Church guided government as well as private life.

The Pilgrims came to America after a century of Protestant reformation, only nine years after the King James translation of the Bible was complete. They landed at Plymouth Rock with a Bible in one hand and their farming tools in the other to begin carving out a new nation. The Puritans followed the Pilgrims largely to flee the repressive measures of the Church of England and live in good conscience before God. Soon the northern colonies were populated with Presbyterians, Methodists, and Quakers, among others. As the fur trade began to flourish, other settlers came for commercial reasons.

As the colonies grew and prospered, the king, who controlled the land grants, began to encourage the Church of England to send Anglican clergymen to the new land. Later on, Catholics began to migrate, settling at first in Maryland, which got its name from "Mary's-Land," referring to the Virgin Mary.

While not all of the colonists were Christians, an overwhelming proportion of them were. Christianity and the Bible permeated their laws, customs, public policy, and culture. During the seventeenth and eighteenth centuries, America was *not* a secular state. Religion was not only indulged, it was promoted by the colonial governments. Although personal faith was not required for citizenship, almost every state constitution required that candidates for public office acknowledge a belief in God and in future rewards and punishments. For example, the constitutions of Pennsylvania and Vermont stated: "And each member, before he takes his seat, shall make and subscribe the following declaration, viz.: 'I do believe in one God, the creator and governor of the universe, the rewarder to the good and the punisher of the wicked.'"[3]

Similarly, the constitution of Tennessee stated: "No person who denies the being of God, or a future state of rewards and punishments, shall hold any office in the civil department of this State."[4]

BENJAMIN FRANKLIN ON THE RELIGIOUS NATURE OF COLONIAL AMERICA

Benjamin Franklin, famous for his practical sayings and proverbs in the popular *Poor Richard's Almanac,* held many high public offices in the government. Though he may not have been a professing Christian, he was respectful toward Christianity. He became a friend of the great evangelist and orator George Whitefield, and many think he may have become a Christian during the Great Awakening.

Because Benjamin Franklin is not clearly known to have been a Christian, his view of the religious faith of the American people in the eighteenth century is particularly interesting. While he was the colonial government's envoy to England, Franklin gave written testimony that atheism—the bedrock of secularism—was little known in the colonies. In his pamphlet *Information to Those Who Would Remove to America*, he wrote:

> *Bad examples to youth are more rare in America, which must be a comfortable consideration to parents. To this may be truly added, that serious religion, under its various denominations, is not only tolerated, but respected and practised. Atheism is unknown there; infidelity rare and secret; so that persons may live to a great age in that country without having their piety shocked by meeting with either an Atheist or an Infidel. And the Divine Being seems to have manifested his approbation of the mutual forbearance and kindness with which the different sects treat each other, by the remarkable prosperity with which he has been pleased to favor the whole country.[5]*

Franklin, whose pamphlet may have been somewhat exaggerated perhaps to promote immigration to America, still obviously believed the nation was not founded or populated by infidels, atheists, or hedonists. Why shouldn't our founding fathers have been religious? America was established largely by immigrants from northern Europe, the area most influenced by the Reformation. Among the more than 3 million Americans at the time of the Revolutionary War and the writing of the Constitution, Protestant Christianity was the dominant religious persuasion.

THE FOUNDING OF THE UNITED STATES OF AMERICA, 1789

After the Revolutionary War, it became obvious that the colonies could not thrive if they existed as thirteen little countries competing with each other. Consequently, to "provide for the national defense and to promote domestic tranquillity"—really the only purpose of a federal government—our founders decided to write a constitution that would be fair to all states, regardless of their size. Congress was to be made up of two houses: the number of delegates in the House of Representatives was based on the population of each state, and each state had two senators to give better representation to all.

Just as the Pilgrims, Puritans, and other Christians believed God had granted them success against overwhelming odds during the Revolutionary War, so they depended upon divine help in drafting what was to be the greatest constitution in the history of the world. Each state elected its best men to represent their values, morals, and beliefs and sent them to Philadelphia to write a national constitution that would embody those beliefs. Most of these men came from states whose people were so opposed to being ruled over by atheists that candidates were obliged to sign a statement testifying to their faith in God. Some had to acknowledge their belief in the Lord Jesus Christ as the Son of God.

These men wrote the Constitution, the foundation of this republic. Written in 1787, it is considered by many to be the greatest governmental document ever written. It has provided more freedom and prosperity for more people than any other constitution in the history of mankind. It established the self-government of a major country by common citizens who vote their leaders into office. And it has survived the longest period—more than two hundred years—of uninterrupted self-government.

The fifty-five writers of our Constitution were bright, educated people, well chosen to represent the citizenry in the founding of this nation. A look into their beliefs, values, and philosophies of life will provide us with important insights into the true roots of our nation.

Seventy-three men were elected by their states to represent them at the Constitutional Convention that met between May 27 and September 17, 1787. Rhode Island so opposed the union that it didn't elect anyone. Consequently, only twelve states provided representation. Fifty-five men convened at one time or another, most of whom made some contribution to the document, but only thirty-nine were on hand to sign the Constitution at its completion. These fifty-five, from a variety of backgrounds, made up this nation's founding fathers.

Of the fifty-five delegates who participated in writing the Constitution, all but three were orthodox members of one of the established Christian denominations. Most were deeply religious, all showed great respect for the Christian traditions of the colonies, and all were significantly influenced in their thinking by biblical values.

Although religious qualifications were not a primary requirement in the selection of delegates to the Constitutional Convention, it is doubtful that any of them would have been elected had they not been members of a traditional religious denomination or at least respectful of the Christian faith.

THE MOST INFLUENTIAL FOUNDING FATHER WAS ABSENT
John Whitehead, founder of the Rutherford Institute, has
said that the most influential man in the writing of our
Constitution was not even present at the Constitutional
Convention—he had died years earlier. His name was John
Calvin.

A great number of the founding fathers were Calvinists,
which may account for our Constitution's ingenious system
of checks and balances. The founding fathers developed this
system because they understood that given man's fallen nature, a president might become a dictator if entirely free to
govern with his power unchecked.

The system of checks and balances was designed to
prevent abuses of power on the part of the executive,
legislative, and judicial branches of government through
mutual accountability. This system worked well until humanistic philosophies over the years became more influential throughout government. Perhaps the most obvious
effect has been the U.S. Supreme Court's turning from
interpreting the Constitution to *making laws.* Today we are
governed by such Supreme Court rulings rather than
through the process of legislation because sometimes federal and state legislatures, as in the case of providing access
to public education for all races, were slow to pass laws that
granted constitutional rights to all its citizens.

With due respect to John Whitehead, we agree that the
most influential man upon our founding fathers was not
present at the drafting of the Constitution, but in our opinion, that man was Rev. John Witherspoon. Dr. Francis
Schaeffer wrote the following of him:

61

John Witherspoon, a Presbyterian minister and president of what is now Princeton University, was the only pastor to sign the Declaration of Independence. He was a very important man during the founding of the country. He linked the Christian thinking represented by the College of New Jersey (now Princeton University) with the work he did both on the Declaration of Independence and on important committees in the founding of the country. This linkage of Christian thinking and the concepts of government were not incidental but fundamental. John Witherspoon knew and stood consciously in the stream of Samuel Rutherford, a Scotsman who lived from 1600–1661 and who wrote Lex Rex *in 1644.* Lex rex *means law is king—a phrase that was absolutely earthshaking. Prior to that it had been* rex lex, *the king is law. In* Lex Rex *he wrote that the law, and no one else, is king. Therefore, the heads of government are under the law, not a law unto themselves.*[6]

John Witherspoon was influential in the writing of our Constitution because nine of the fifty-five men who helped draft the Constitution were his legal disciples. They had learned their view of law from him in small classes at the College of New Jersey. He indoctrinated them in the legal concepts of William Blackstone, a dedicated Christian whose books on law were the cornerstone of the American legal system until they were replaced during this century by the works of humanistic liberals who control the bulk of today's law schools.

One of these nine disciples of the Presbyterian minister/legal expert John Witherspoon was James Madison, called "the father of the Constitution." At thirty-six, he was the most prepared, having just won a legal battle to overturn the state church of Virginia and establish a bill of rights guaranteeing religious freedom for his state. Since he wrote the Bill of Rights for our Constitution, it is not surprising that the First Amendment guarantees religious freedom, for his life's passion was to enforce the belief that government should not dictate what religion a citizen accepts but protect the citizen's right to live according to personal conscience and faith.

MADISON ON RELIGION'S PLACE IN SOCIETY

Some think Madison's passion for religious freedom was sparked when as a boy he and his father overheard shouting coming from the city jail in their hometown of Orange, Virginia. As they listened to imprisoned Baptist ministers whose sole crime was preaching without a state-granted license, young James's father, a dedicated Christian, commented that ministers should never be imprisoned for preaching the gospel in a free country.

Those words and that experience burned the importance of religious freedom into James Madison's heart and had no small influence on the state of religion in our nation. In fact, Madison's First Amendment provided our nation's guarantee of religious freedom until it was turned upside down during this century by the ACLU and liberal lawyers who were appointed to the United States Supreme Court.

Since the writing of our Constitution, our religious liberties have been systematically threatened and whittled away by Supreme Court justices who interpret the First Amendment as a prohibition against religious activity on public property.

Even public prayer has been erroneously labeled unconstitutional.

Since James Madison was the father of the Constitution, he is eminently qualified to define what he and the framers meant when they wrote it:

> *Religion, or the duty we owe to our Creator, and the manner of discharging it, can be directed only by reason and conviction, not by force or violence; and, therefore, that all men should enjoy the fullest toleration in the exercise of religion according to the dictates of conscience, unpunished and unrestrained by the magistrate, unless under color of religion any man disturb the peace, the happiness, or safety of society, and that is the mutual duty of all to practice Christian forbearance, love, and charity toward each other.*[7]

THE CONSTITUTIONS OF ALL FIFTY STATES ACKNOWLEDGE GOD

Another evidence of the strong religious consensus of America's founders appears in all thirteen of the original state constitutions. Each state's constitutional document refers to almighty God as the author of liberty and mentions their dependence on his providence to sustain them as a free people.

Consider some of these inspiring preambles:

North Carolina, 1868
> *We the people of the State of North Carolina, grateful to Almighty God, the sovereign ruler of nations, for the preservation of the American Union and the existence of our civil, political, and religious liberties, and acknowledging our de-*

pendence upon Him for the continuance of those blessings to us and our posterity, do, for the more certain security thereof and for the better government of this State, ordain and establish this constitution.

New Jersey, 1844

We, the people of the State of New Jersey, grateful to Almighty God for the civil and religious liberty which He hath so long permitted us to enjoy, and looking to Him for a blessing upon our endeavors to secure and transmit the same unimpaired to succeeding generations, do ordain and establish this Constitution.

Rhode Island, 1842

We, the people of the State of Rhode Island and Providence Plantations, grateful to Almighty God for the civil and religious liberty which He hath so long permitted us to enjoy, and looking to Him for a blessing upon our endeavors to secure and to transmit the same unimpaired to succeeding generations, do ordain and establish this constitution of government.

New York, 1846

We, the people of the State of New York, grateful to Almighty God for our freedom: in order to secure its blessings, do establish this Constitution.

Did you wonder at the dates? To stress their universal acknowledgment of God as protector, provider, and guide, these examples were all updated *after* the founding fathers were dead, indicating clearly that the consensus of reliance on God, so common at the founding of the nation, was still very much alive several generations later.

Even more interesting is a fact brought to light by the well-known Presbyterian pastor and television minister Dr. James Kennedy in a sermon on the subject of church and state:

> *In reading over the Constitutions of all fifty of our states, I discovered something which some of you may not know: there is in all fifty, without exception, an appeal or a prayer to the Almighty God of this universe. . . . Through all fifty state Constitutions, without exception, there runs this same appeal and reference to God who is the Creator of our liberties and the preserver of our freedoms.[8]*

We find it strange that all the constitutions of all the states acknowledge God, yet our youngest citizens cannot offer public prayer to him in our public schools. At a time when a frightening number of our nation's youth have chosen to adopt the cultural values of barbarians instead of those of our founding fathers, it is time to examine whether we have been subtly secularized by those who do not share those values. Certainly the founding fathers would not object to acknowledging God and his values, for they proudly admitted they were a religious people.

The Printing of Bibles by the First Congress

The Bible, the Word of God, and by popular admission the greatest book ever written, is indispensable to the preservation of Christianity. That fact was made clear in the first act of Congress, authorizing the printing of twenty thousand Bibles for the Indians.[9] In order to unify our people, our leaders sought for the universal acceptance of and access to the Word of God.

Today if Congress authorized the printing of Bibles for people in Bosnia, the ACLU and others would scream, "What about the separation of church and state!" Our founding fathers showed no reluctance in favoring Christianity, the commonly practiced religion of their day. Evidently, they didn't see this act as imposing a religion on people but rather as promoting morality in the fledgling nation.

RELIGION IN AMERICA FIFTY YEARS
AFTER THE CONSTITUTION

French scholar and historian Alexis de Tocqueville visited America in 1831. He was so impressed with our culture and constitutional system that he published an exhaustive, two-volume description of our nation that is still popular and available. The following are some of his observations on the religious life of the nation:

> *On my arrival in the United States the religious aspect of the country was the first thing that struck my attention; and the longer I stayed there, the more I perceived the great political consequences resulting from this new state of religion and the spirit of freedom marching in opposite directions. But in America I found they were intimately united and that they reigned in common over the same country. . . .*
>
> *Religion in America takes no part in the government of*

society, but it must be regarded as the first of their political institutions; for if it does not impart a taste for freedom, it facilitates the use of it. Indeed, it is in this same point of view that the inhabitants of the United States themselves look upon religious belief. I do not know whether all Americans have a sincere faith in their religion—for who can search the human heart?—But I am certain that they hold it to be indispensable to the maintenance of republican institutions. This opinion is not peculiar to a class of citizens or a party, but it belongs to the whole nation and to every rank of society. . . .

The sects that exist in the United States are innumerable. . . . Moreover, all the sects of the United States are comprised within the great unity of Christianity, and Christian morality is everywhere the same.

In the United States the sovereign authority is religious, and consequently hypocrisy must be common: but there is no country in the world where the Christian religion retains a greater influence over the souls of men than in America; and there can be no greater proof of its utility and of its conformity to human nature than that its influence is powerfully felt over the most enlightened and free nation of the earth.

In the United States the influence of religion is not confined to the manners, but it extends to the intelligence of the people. Among the Anglo-Americans some profess the doctrines of Christianity from a sincere belief in them, and others do the same because they fear to be suspected of unbelief. Christianity, therefore, reigns without obstacle, by universal consent; the consequence is, as I have before observed, that every principle of the moral world is fixed and determinate, although the political world is abandoned to the debates and the experiments of men. Thus the human mind is never left to wander over a boundless field.[10]

It would be difficult to exaggerate the influence of the Bible and the church on the writing of the amazing document we call the Constitution of the United States. It could never have been produced by an amoral or biblically illiterate people.

OUR FIRST JUSTICE OF THE SUPREME COURT

John Jay, like Thomas Jefferson, was out of the country at the time our Constitution was written. He was our envoy to England, Jefferson our envoy to France. Jay returned home just in time to become one of the three men who wrote the *Federalist Papers,* without which the new Constitution would never have been adopted by the states. He was selected by George Washington as the first chief justice of the Supreme Court.

John Jay believed not only that Americans were a religious people, but he also believed—like many others who were influential people in our nation's founding—that America was a Christian nation. His words seem almost foreign in view of today's secularized climate: "Providence has given to our people the choice of their rulers," wrote Jay, "and it is the duty, as well as the privilege and interest, of a Christian nation to select and prefer Christians for their rulers."[11]

It is easy for any unbiased investigator to see that this nation was founded by a religious people, most of whom were Christians. Our nation's laws and our public schools were established according to Judeo-Christian principles (laws and principles that came down to us from Mount Sinai and the

Mount of Olives), and public policy reflected the Christian worldview ingrained in our national conscience.

America's Conscience Sustained Us
in the "Good Old Days"

They [the founding fathers] proclaimed to all the world the revolutionary doctrine of the divine rights of the common man. That doctrine has ever since been the heart of the American faith. . . . Recognition of the supreme Being is the first, the most basic, expression of Americanism. Without God, there could be no American form of government, nor American way of life.—Dwight D. Eisenhower[12]

If you're fond of looking back on the good old days of forty or fifty years ago, you're in danger of being ridiculed by those who have a running romance with this new-and-improved, politically correct generation. Admittedly, some things about the good old days really weren't so good. For example, once it took six to eight weeks to travel across America. Who wouldn't prefer jetting across the country? We are both very grateful that it's possible to speak in Florida on Friday and Saturday and in California on Sunday. Without any question, most technological progress beats the old days' alternatives.

But in those good old days there existed in this country a wholesome kind of lifestyle that certainly was superior to what we have today. Such expressions as "A man's word is his bond" or "You are your brother's keeper" lent themselves to a richer, more humane way of life. Marriage was most often a commitment for life, divorce rates were low, and single-parent

70

families were rare. Children usually grew up with the security of both parents at home.

Our streets were safe day and night. Murder, rape, and mayhem were the exception, not the rule. There was, in fact, a "Christian consensus" in this country that produced a basic respect for one's fellowman, making life safe and enjoyable.

But today, in certain big cities, when you say good-bye to your loved ones each morning, you have no assurance that you will see them again. Ask any of the nine families in New York City who experienced the loss of a loved one when an armed madman shot blindly through a subway train as people were on their way home from work. In a single moment of time, countless families' lives were changed forever.

Or consider the Washington, D.C., parents of a seventeen-year-old honor student whose jealous boyfriend blew her brains out in a "lovers' quarrel." They would probably trade modernity for the good old days when our streets were safe.

EVEN DETROIT STREETS WERE SAFE

Both of us grew up in the city of Detroit, Michigan, "the motor car capital of the world." A few years ago Tim was reminiscing about his boyhood and asked his mother about her life during his childhood. She had raised three children as a single parent after Tim's father died suddenly following a heart attack.

Tim's mother told him that because the family hadn't lived in the county for eighteen months (a requirement in those days), the family didn't qualify for welfare even though the youngest child was only seven weeks old—Tim's sister was five, and Tim himself was only ten. Consequently, the entire family became workaholics just to survive. As the old adage says, "Necessity is the mother of invention."

So instead of government aid, Tim and his family depended on relatives. His aunt and her family of four took them into their two-bedroom house for the first year. Tim's mother got a job in a factory working the afternoon shift from three to midnight so they could eventually move into a rented apartment. When Tim asked his mother if she was frightened to ride the city bus between 12:00 and 1:00 A.M. each night, she said, "It never occurred to me that a woman wasn't safe on the streets of Detroit after dark!"

As a young teenage girl living in Highland Park, a suburb of Detroit, Beverly was able to get a part-time job during the Christmas season as a cashier in a nearby jewelry store. Every evening when the store closed at 9:00 P.M., she would have a seven-block walk down Woodward Avenue to her street and then another block to her home. It was always dark at that hour, and some areas were dimly lit. But there was never any question of danger because the streets were safe, even after dark.

How times have changed! No woman in her right mind would imitate our younger lifestyles today because America's cities have become a battle zone. Twenty-three thousand people are murdered on our city streets each year. And crime isn't limited to adults. Our schools report more than a quarter of a million acts of violence each year, making violence a parent's number one fear as children go off to school.

In his report on the cultural decline of America, Dr. William Bennett pointed out that the major problems in public schools in the 1940s were talking in class, chewing gum, skipping school, and not getting homework in on time. But in the 1990s, our schools' top problems are guns in the classroom, forcible rape, and gang-related violence. We think another top problem is a school curriculum that includes sex education materials explicit enough to make a stevedore blush. Some of these courses contain teaching diametrically opposed to the values of the parents, who pay the salaries of the teachers and the cost of sex education materials with taxes but have virtually no control over what is taught in school.

SEX EDUCATION IN THE GOOD OLD DAYS

As a boy in the ninth grade, Tim received on one afternoon all the sex education he needed to prepare him for life—including life in the military and until marriage. Some boy in the class said a dirty word in the locker room and was overheard by the coach, the most respected faculty member of Tim's school. Coach marched the boys to the gym, where they were seated on the floor. They never touched a basketball that day. They listened to that good man—a father of seven—while he lectured them about sex.

Tim says he can still see Coach in his maroon school sweatshirt and white shorts, the whistle around his neck swinging back and forth as he forcefully preached about boys, girls, responsibility, respect for the opposite sex, virtue, self-respect, self-control, and lots of morality!

That was the best sex-ed talk Tim ever heard. The coach never hesitated to impose his moral values. He taught America's moral ideals to all his students because basic morality shouldn't offend anyone, no matter what religion you are. On that day there was no ACLU screaming "separation of church and state." People for the Atheist Way, who presumptuously call themselves People for the American Way, were not there to censor the coach and accuse him of being a "right-wing fundamentalist." If they had, they would have been stoned by the parents who were thrilled that their children were given that kind of moral instruction by a good role model. Tim's coach taught the Christian consensus of morality that was nearly universal back then.

In the good old days that were as recent as our adolescence, only rarely did a girl in high school become pregnant. In fact, as a teenage girl in a large Michigan public high school, Beverly was not aware of any girls who became pregnant while still in high school. She, too, had teachers who held up a standard of morality.

Today, however, Tim's coach would be fired by many school boards if he delivered such a morally committed lecture. A vast gulf of difference exists between education then and our current educational system, where educators insist upon a purely secular education that centers on man, not God, and curriculum material that teaches that moral absolutes don't exist.

Today's schools have fostered an obsession with sex that has resulted in a tenfold increase in adolescent sexual activity, teenage pregnancy, and rape, while millions of adult Americans cannot read well enough to hold a job where reading is required. Instead of facing the fact that they are doing a very poor job of teaching Johnny to read, our public school officials are busy establishing school-based sex clinics that pass out condoms. In so doing, they are legitimating promiscuity and exacerbating the problem.

Through the activities of Concerned Women for America, Beverly has actively challenged taxpayers to be involved and have an influence with the public school classroom. The children at risk are *our children,* and we pay the taxes that support the schools. Our schools need an old-fashioned dose of morality, but modern *educrats* refuse to provide anything that depends upon a universal moral code.

OUR NATION TODAY

One Sunday morning as Tim drove through Washington, D.C., he was struck with the thought that our nation's capital is an apt analogy of what's happening to America today. Aside from the national monuments in Washington, the city is not a pretty sight. Trash blows down the streets, windows are boarded up, sleazy neon signs blink and advertise XXX-rated films and girlie shows from the curbside, and small groups of teens hang out in doorways while police patrol the streets. But far behind the rubbish you can still see the Victorian elegance of what were once lovely homes and elegant buildings.

You would think that our nation's capital would remain clean, orderly, and exemplary regardless of what happens to the rest of the country. After all, don't the monuments inspire awe and remind us of our forefathers' high aspirations, courage, sacrifice, and moral standards? Why is it then that Washington, D.C., is the "murder capital" of the world? Why was the former mayor of our nation's historic capital promptly elected for another city post following his prison term for cocaine possession?

Why are we surprised to see rampant crime and the valuing of possessions over people? As C. S. Lewis observed in *The*

Abolition of Man (New York: Macmillan, 1955), "In a sort of ghastly simplicity we remove the organ and demand the function. We make men without chests and expect of them virtue and enterprise. We laugh at honor and are shocked to find traitors in our midst. We castrate and bid the geldings be fruitful" (p. 35).

We are observing in our nation the consequences of turning away from God. The words *In God We Trust* inscribed in our currency no longer represent a national reality. The truth of the matter is that "in man we trust." And, as we are learning painfully, man's ways are no substitute for God's. "'For My thoughts are not your thoughts, neither are your ways My ways,' declares the Lord. 'For as the heavens are higher than the earth, so are My ways higher than your ways, and My thoughts than your thoughts'" (Isa. 55:8-9).

One needs only look at statistics to see how much our nation's moral landscape has changed. In Washington, D.C., murder, rape, and burglary have increased dramatically in the last few years. Sadly, much of the rise in crime must be attributed to the government's welfare policy, which has taught that individuals thrive not through hard work but through government subsidies. Quick money has become the name of the game, and drug trade pays too well for many to resist.

George Washington once observed that "few men have the virtue to withstand the highest bidder."[13] Why should a teenage boy work for minimum wage at the local grocery when he can make big bucks in a few minutes selling drugs? But the wisdom of darkness will fade in the harsh reality of daylight when his lifeless body is found among the litter of the streets, leaving behind his mourning mother, sisters, and brothers.

Washington, D.C., is only an analogy of the bigger picture of what is happening in America. Death and destruction are on the rise, life and production on the wane. The good old days have passed into oblivion as our nation's conscience has failed.

Aleksandr Solzhenitsyn, deeply acquainted with the destruction of the human soul, has said that this century's slaughter and brutality must be attributed to the transfer of trust in God to trust in man. "The failings of human consciousness, deprived of its divine dimension, have been a determining factor in all the major crimes of our present century."[14]

Were people different in the good old days? Some blame America's contemporary problems—drugs, shootings, teen pregnancy, poverty, despair, absentee fathers, the family breakdown—on "the way people are today." In reality, however, people today are no worse than they were in the previous generation. Since Adam, each of us has inherited the same propensity to indulge our selfish desires regardless of the consequences our actions may have on those around us. The difference between the people of this violent, uncommitted, despairing generation and those of earlier days is not to be found in our internal makeup. Rather, it can be found in the lack of moral consensus and the resistance to higher morality in education, the media, and the government, leading them to make incessant demands for rights without responsibilities.

Christian financial counselor and author Larry Burkett writes about his experience growing up in the 1950s:

We weren't better kids back then, even though I never knew anyone who used drugs, carried a gun to school, or beat up a teacher. We simply were held in check by a society that had enough common sense to realize that we needed to be controlled for our own good. . . .

I grieve when I think what it must be like for teenagers today, with hardly any restraints on their actions. Even worse, our society is telling them they should have no restraints. I know I pushed the boundaries of our restraints back then; fortunately, they were a lot more confining.[15]

These restraints—laws of morality—were effective because the foundation supporting them was strong and widely accepted. Certainly not all Americans were Christians in previous generations, but the foundations laid in America's early, formative days were based upon the biblical teaching that fallen man was prone to sin and consequently needed to be held in check by just laws. Humanistic reasoning in the past two centuries, in contrast, has promoted the entirely unfounded belief that man was basically good and tended to do good. It was society and its institutions, humanists claimed, that corrupted man.

Justice was different, therefore, in the good old days. Because the American system of government was based upon an understanding of man's nature from a biblical perspective, it was able to anticipate sin in its many forms and develop ways to curtail its advance in the nation.

The examples of today's skewed justice are numerous: Take, for instance, the Reginald Denny case in which the would-be murderer brutally beat a man for no apparent reason except race. Videotape left no doubt regarding the defendant's guilt. However, the jury gave the remorseless defendant a light sentence.

In a similar case, which ended in the death of the victim, the defendant gloated, "I loved watching the blood gush from [the victim's] eyes."[16] This man, who, as in the Reginald Denny case, showed no remorse, was sent to a judge who insisted that the case concerned not only homicide but also "social awareness." Unbelievably, the judge made the following statement in *defense* of the murderer:

> *This killing was effectuated to focus attention on a chronic and pervasive illness of racial discrimination and of hurt, sorrow, and rejection. Throughout Dougan's [the murderer's] life, his resentment to bias and prejudice festered. . . . The victim was a symbolic representative of the class causing the perceived injustices.*[17]

"Justice" was not always designed to protect the guilty and hurt the innocent. Larry Burkett, who grew up poor, observes wistfully that justice was once grounded on a firm, secure, equitable foundation. Justice was "just": "If I had burned down a neighbor's home," writes Burkett, "I don't think the courts of the fifties would have cared much that I had grown up underprivileged; but that was when the courts still administered biblical justice instead of social values."[18]

What were American schools like in the good old days? Until thirty years ago, each school day began with prayer— something like this prayer that was banned in *Engel v. Vitale* in 1962:

Almighty God, we acknowledge our dependence upon Thee, and we beg Thy blessings upon us, our parents, our teachers, and our country.

Tim remembers his elementary schoolteacher keeping order in the lunchroom. Before anyone opened his or her lunch pail, a simple prayer of thanks was said by a student or the teacher.

God was openly acknowledged and called upon in public schools and in public life. Family, schools, and government were committed to him at the beginning of the school day. Students learned to acknowledge God and to be thankful for what they had. And God watched over our families, protecting our nation from the ravages of crime, abuse, and STDs, and we enjoyed high esteem in the sight of other nations, according to God's promise in Psalm 91:14-16: "I will protect him, for he acknowledges my name. He will call upon me, and I will answer him; I will be with him in trouble, I will deliver him and honor him. With long life will I satisfy him and show him my salvation" (NIV).

The recent shooting of three boys in their Washington, D.C., high school hallway by another student and the violence committed against patrolling police officers have moved many in Congress to call for prayer in schools. Even D.C.'s former mayor has called for the return of prayer to our schools in the hope that it would return peace to the classrooms, like it was in the good old days before secularists destroyed the Judeo-Christian moral consensus in this country.

In 1993 a federal appeals court in Houston, Texas, ruled that while the Constitution bars school officials from initiating prayer, it does not stop students from praying. Lawmakers in at least nine states are following Texas's lead: Legislatures in Georgia, Alabama, Tennessee, Mississippi, and Virginia have passed measures authorizing student-led prayer at school events. Similar bills are pending in South Carolina, Louisiana, and Oklahoma. (The Florida legislature killed its version of the bill.)

Pat Robertson's American Center for Law and Justice has initiated a campaign to educate students about their constitutional right to pray and speak about God, but the battle is far from over. The American Civil Liberties Union is waging a vigorous countercampaign. Upon what grounds? "This is an incredibly well-coordinated campaign," said Phil Gutis, an ACLU official in New York. "They can talk about this being led by students, but the religious right is spending millions of dollars to reintroduce prayer into the schools."[19]

WHAT WE CAN DO

There are attempts to return to our roots of righteousness, but never has the battle against such a return been so vigorous. America has not always been a sterling example of justice and well-being for all, for sin is a force to be dealt with in every society. Nevertheless, righteousness was never resisted as fervently as it is today. Habitual sin was not openly promoted as a lifestyle in previous generations as it is today. While the vices committed today are nothing new ("There is nothing new under the sun"—Ecclesiastes 1:9), in the good old days people viewed vice as a shameful thing. Today shame is related to the religious right or those who would impose their moral values on others.

Just think a moment—when is the last time you heard anyone say, "Aren't you ashamed of yourself?" Shame is the natural result of a quickened conscience, and our lack of shame testifies eloquently to the silencing of the powerful and God-fearing conscience that was instrumental in the forming of our great nation.

It is time for individuals, families, and churches to allow another voice to be heard, uncompromised by our own inconsistencies. We can't criticize the effects of public television if we keep the TV sets turned on all day. We can't criticize non-Christian or anti-Christian teaching in public schools if we don't support Christian private schools or make our voices heard before school boards and in the voting booth.

> *A mental possession of ours which enables us to pass some sort of judgment, correct or mistaken, upon moral questions as they arise. . . . Your conscience is simply that ideal of life which constitutes your moral personality.—Josiah Royce, 1908*[20]

our
conscience
seared:

4

It is astonishing how soon the whole conscience begins to unravel
if a single stitch drops. One single sin indulged in makes
a hole you could put your head through.

CHARLES BUXTON[1]

In vain we call old notions fudge,
And bend our conscience to our dealing;
The Ten Commandments will not budge,
And stealing will continue stealing.

JAMES RUSSELL LOWELL[2]

Depending on their training and temperament, people feel varying degrees of guilt when they do wrong. If they are raised in a relativistic culture that has no place for right and wrong but believes that whatever seems good to the individual is OK, their natural conscience will be weakened or even "seared." In the fourth chapter of 1 Timothy, the apostle Paul refers to people who will fall away from the faith as being "seared in their own conscience as with a branding iron" (4:2).

THE DECLINE OF THE AMERICAN CONSCIENCE

As the church has ceased to be the most influential guide in the molding of our national conscience, every moral value of the past has been assaulted. The evidence surrounds us—consider profanity, for example. Not too long ago, the "d" word was rarely used in public, but today the "f" word falls off the tongues of adults as if it were part of proper speech.

At first the entertainment industry ignored morals; now morality is openly attacked. Once our nation looked to religious leaders like Billy Graham, Bishop J. Fulton Sheen, and Rabbi Tannenbaum to set community standards, but today filthy-mouthed "comics" like Roseanne Arnold or talk-show hosts like Howard Stern are imitated as though their standards of right and wrong were "gospel."

Clearly a widespread assault is being waged on the morals of millions of school children by adults who insist that old moral values should be replaced by the "new morality." This "new morality" is based on relativism (nothing is absolutely right or wrong; choices depend on your situation), which inevitably deals a death blow to the social conscience.

A pastor friend of ours told us about a twenty-one-year-old college girl from his church who came to ask his advice. When the pastor learned that the girl was living with a young man, his face revealed his deep disappointment and surprise. At this, the young woman nonchalantly replied, "Pastor, being a virgin is no big deal anymore."

We know we are in bad shape when people who have been reared in the church feel no remorse for their immoral lifestyles. Just a generation ago a woman living with a man who was not her husband would certainly not have been respectable.

According to the latest surveys, our society has made promiscuity morally acceptable, for 51 percent of girls and 67 percent of boys are said to be sexually active before they graduate from high school. After high school, unless they marry young, the promiscuity level goes off the chart. Sexually transmitted diseases (STDs) and the incurable AIDS plague are evidence that chastity is a thing of the past for most young people. There is, however, a growing positive movement to restore virtue and chastity among our young people. Both Protestant and Catholic churches have launched national campaigns to urge young people to remain chaste until marriage.

While religious leaders and parents are encouraging young people to engrave the biblical mandate for sexual purity in their conscience, government officials and educators are, through neglect or in the name of avoiding religion-based moralities, accommodating promiscuity, causing the consciences of our youth to be seared. Some government agencies provide free condoms for teens, with or without parental permission. The government, while allowing abortion clinics to operate, is mostly silent about the need for courses that stress abstinence before marriage or teach why and how young people should say no.

When Concerned Women for America released *Wait for Me,* a video for teens that promotes waiting until marriage for sex, the video won four national awards and one international award because it carried the unique message that virtue is important and a better way of life. Why has our government failed to give this welcome message to our children? Beverly received many letters from teens who saw this moving video. There were many who stated they wished they could have seen this video (of waiting until marriage to engage in sex) before they had become sexually active. Some were thirteen- to fourteen-year-old girls. Our government has deceived these young people by lying to them, telling them that sex before marriage is safe if you simply use a condom. Many girls will carry the scars from this message to their grave.

LEGALIZING IMMORALITY

The greatest moral blight on our governmental and educational leaders—particularly our judges—is the legalization of abortion. Ever since the *Roe v. Wade* ruling by the Supreme Court in 1973, our society has cheapened the value of human life to the point that we are now beginning to talk about legalizing euthanasia. As Dr. Francis Schaeffer used to point out, some fear that it won't be long until our elderly will see the doctor coming with a syringe and wonder if the injection is intended to make him better or to take his life.

We take no joy in pointing out how harmful homosexuality is from a biblical or physiological position. We both have spent considerable time studying the subject. Tim has written a book to help homosexuals. We believe there is hope through faith in Jesus Christ for these tormented people—they can come out of the homosexual lifestyle. We have seen many of them set free from what may be the most powerful vice. But before a man or woman can be freed, he or she must be willing to admit that homosexuality is wrong and seek God's help in finding victory.

Claiming only a desire to show fairness to all segments of the population, our government protects homosexuals and has even changed its laws to accommodate them. Despite the claims, it appears that the government does not want to give homosexuals *equal* rights—they end up giving them *special* rights. We have established "hate crime" laws that forbid (in a land that has prided itself on freedom of speech) public condemnation of this dangerous lifestyle. Hospitals are not supposed to warn doctors before surgery when a patient has AIDS. At the time of this writing, a dentist was being sued for transferring an AIDS patient to a university's specially equipped AIDS ward because the homosexual patient demanded that he be treated as a "normal" person. He was anything but normal; he was dying from AIDS and was a threat to the dentist as well as to every other patient that dentist would treat.

THE GUILTY HAVE BECOME VICTIMS

The most secular discipline in education today is the field of psychiatry. Many of its most influential leaders have been anti-Christian and antimoral. Their attack on morals is legendary. During the past fifty years psychiatrists have waged a running war against the conscience.

Most psychiatrists and psychologists have been confronted with the fact that a high percentage of their patients experience heavy guilt. Since humanistic psychology is committed to evolution as an explanation for man's origin, most mental health professionals believe that man is born neutral and his conscience is molded by his environment. Guilt, therefore, is the result of environmental damage.

Christians, on the other hand, understand that when a human being violates his conscience, his experience with guilt is a good, healthy response. Regret and sorrow may lead to repentance, forgiveness, and a renewed relationship with God.

If psychiatrists could do away with the conscience, they would strike a powerful blow against Christianity, for the law and our consciences through the ministry of the Holy Spirit—inspired preaching of the Word of God, have a "convicting" effect on people. It is conscience that leads men and women to call out to God through his Son for forgiveness.

The very best therapy for a guilty conscience is not drug therapy, shock therapy, or labeling the conscience as "misguided religious teaching from your youth." The best therapy is a genuine conversion experience with Jesus Christ who, as we shall see, offers a clean conscience.

John MacArthur has dealt quite thoroughly with this in his book *The Vanishing Conscience*. MacArthur points out that humanistic psychology's assault on the human conscience has turned guilty sinners into victims of society. (It isn't *your* fault that you got drunk and killed three people driving under the influence of alcohol. Blame the alcohol or the bartender who didn't stop serving you—but don't blame yourself.) If a person turns out to be a homosexual serial killer, as the recent case in Wisconsin, it isn't his fault. Psychologists say he was genetically or socially driven to perform such acts as homosexual rape, sodomy, cannibalism, and murder.

In the last two years the American public has been treated to bizarre court decisions that have shown callous disregard for the injured and treated the guilty as victims. The jurors of the famous Menendez brothers could not find the brothers guilty even though they admitted to shooting their parents. They were victims. At twenty and twenty-two years of age?

No one seems willing to take the blame for anything today. We have no-fault divorce, no-fault insurance, no-fault *anything*, unless it's something the government deems objectionable. As MacArthur points out, officialdom has done away with sin—abortion, adultery, fornication, homosexuality, you name it—unless it is something for which they can exact taxes, such as alcohol and tobacco. Then they are willing to call it "a sin tax."

OUR LEADERS HAVE LOST THEIR CONSCIENCE

The president of the United States has traditionally been the defender and executor of moral values. But despite his campaign for "family values," Mr. Clinton's first acts in office revealed his insensitivity toward those who hold to traditional family values as he struck down all executive orders against abortion and tried to open the way to allow gays in the military with no restriction. His approval of homosexuality as a credible lifestyle is seen in his appointment of more homosexuals to his government than any other president in history.

Another blatant attack on traditional moral values occurred when the people of the state of Colorado passed an amendment to their constitution prohibiting homosexuals from receiving "special rights," such as those of marriage and adoption. Constitutionally, "Amendment Two," as it is called, should be the law in that state today, but at this writing it has been held up more than two years because a judge who favors special privileges to gays has overthrown it. For all practical purposes, he has put himself above the people of his state, having defied both the will of the people who pay his salary and the intent of the Constitution that he swore to uphold. In addition, the equally liberal governor and his attorney general both oppose Amendment Two, favoring the granting of special rights to the gay community. They refuse to use the resources of their state government to overturn the judge's decision and enact the law.

This kind of judicial dictatorship is not unique to the state of Colorado. It happens in many states and in our federal government. Recently, in *NOW v. Scheidler*, the Supreme Court declared that the RICO Act (Racketeer Influenced Corrupt Organizations), designed to imprison drug traffickers and criminals, applies to pro-lifers who demonstrate in front of abortion clinics. The secularizers who run this country will not rest until they destroy all morality with which they disagree—virtually everything necessary to the conduct of a safe and morally sound society.

Violence and Vulgarity in Entertainment

We can see how badly our nation's conscience has been seared by analyzing the popularity of our morally degenerate entertainment industry. In a free market economy, the entertainment industry would not survive without a sufficient number of people watching television programs, attending movies, and purchasing videos. And in today's market, sex sells. Vulgarity and perversion make money. Violence keeps 'em coming back for sequels. Only recently, after the success of *Aladdin* and *Beauty and the Beast,* has Hollywood even begun to consider that family fare might be worth pursuing.

The Basic Issues of Morality

Morality is not based upon a single issue; a nation cannot declare itself a moral country by adhering to a single moral practice. After all, God himself gave ten moral commandments and scores of statutes, laws, and precepts to the nation of Israel. There are two moral values, however, without which no nation can consider itself moral.

Human Life: Written into our Declaration of Independence is the statement that all men are born possessing "unalienable rights, that among these are life, liberty and the pursuit of happiness." The first and most basic of these rights is life! The founding fathers revered liberty and happiness, but they listed life first because the primary purpose of government is to preserve the lives of its citizens by protecting them wherever possible from violent criminals and foreign oppressors.

As everyone in this country knows, the Supreme Court has ruled that the unalienable right to life for the unborn is superseded by a woman's right "to choose." In other words, we have made an immoral act legal by officially declaring that the choice of the mother—however trivial her reason for destroying her unborn child—takes precedence over her child's right to life.

On April 13, 1994, Senator Bob Packwood appeared on *Good Morning, America.* The host, Charles Gibson, asked the senator how he felt about those in the Senate who wanted to reprimand him for his alleged improper activities with women. Packwood said that he certainly would not enjoy a reprimand, but he wanted people to remember the good things he had done while in office. A few years before *Roe v. Wade,* he told Gibson, he had written "pro-choice" legislation, and not one other congressman would join him in sponsoring the bill!

Unfortunately, we're not the only nation that kills its most innocent citizens. In the name of "population control," the Chinese *require* the abortion of any unborn children a mother may conceive after the birth of her first child. While we are not yet mandating abortion in the United States, our laws grant mothers the right to murder their children for virtually any reason.

It is important to point out that the American people seem to be more morally minded in this regard than their elected leaders. While pro-choice groups claim the opposite result, most polls indicate that the American people still disapprove of abortion on demand. Specifically, 83 percent oppose the use of abortion as a method of birth control, and 56 percent oppose abortion for any reason other than for saving the life of the mother, rape, or incest.[3] When considering the basic moral value of human life, most Americans are morally healthier than their leaders.

Proverbs 17:15 tells us, "Acquitting the guilty and condemning the innocent—the Lord detests them both" (NIV), and yet our nation's leaders favor abortion on demand and oppose the death penalty for convicted murderers (former Supreme Court Justice Blackmun, for example). Our judges have created a judicial mess that frees murderers in such numbers that second-offense murderers exceed the number who should have been executed by due process of law. Again, the government is out of step with God's laws and the will of the people. Why? Because our government is dominated by men and women who have no regard for God or his moral values. Millions of innocent children will die because of their secularist thinking.

Family: The second value that distinguishes a moral nation from a barbaric one is the esteem it holds for the family and sexual expression. The sex drive has always been one of mankind's strongest, taking second place only to the survival instinct. For the proper release of the sex drive, God instituted marriage and designed it for two people of the opposite sex. From as far back as we can go in human history—indeed, back to Adam and Eve—marriage has been the proper channel for the sex drive, both for the bonding of the husband and wife in love and for the propagation of the human race.

We can also trace the *misuse* of the sex drive back to the beginning of recorded history. Prostitution is not called "the oldest profession" for no reason. But moral nations have laws against prostitution, adultery, sodomy, and other distortions of the sex drive. Nations that abolish laws favoring marriage, family, and fidelity do so at their peril. Not only does sexual profligacy afflict individual families—our current divorce rate leaves children angry, hurt, and emotionally impaired—but immoral sexual behavior has historically introduced and spread social diseases.

WHAT HAPPENED TO DECENCY LAWS?

Secularists have always taken a relaxed attitude toward marriage and sexual fidelity, as did Voltaire, Rousseau, and other molders of secular thought. And so it is today. The secularists of our day have simplified the divorce laws to such a level that they have encouraged an epidemic of divorces. Society as a whole refuses to face the fact that divorce causes great harm. Even Christians refuse to accept the fact that a violation of marriage vows made before a holy God reveals a serious character flaw.

Men and women whose consciences have been seared have insisted on and succeeded in overturning decency laws that once prohibited the publication of pornography. Now pornography is a booming business with revenues of more than $10 billion a year. Like a child who plays with matches and gasoline, our nation toys with pornography, never considering its destructive and dangerous potential. Despite the claims of liberal legislators, insisting on First Amendment rights for publishers, pornographic literature does pour emotional gasoline on the vulnerable, leading to a devastating increase in rape, incest, child molestation, and sexual violence at levels unprecedented in this country. And as we write this, government leaders grow more and more quiet about the wrongfulness of sodomy and lesbianism. If the public does not cry out, laws against incest and pedophilia may be the next moral standards to fall.

We are indeed a nation without a conscience!

The guilt associated with abortion, divorce, and adultery has sent millions of Americans rushing to their psychotherapists' offices. Those who promote "choice," open marriage, and divorce rarely admit, much less discuss, the consequences of immoral actions. We have both counseled enough people to understand how great is the sorrow of conscience when a man or woman breaks God's moral law and bears the consequences of conscience. Guilt from an abortion or adultery, inscribed painfully on the table of the human heart, is not easily dismissed. Planned Parenthood and government apologists would do well to admit that these actions cause great emotional distress.

WHEN DID AMERICA STOP HEEDING HER CONSCIENCE?

Dr. Francis Schaeffer once said that during the 1880s secular humanism triumphed in Europe over the remains of the Reformation-period revivals. Then he added, "America, because of her heavier biblical grid, did not cross that line of despair until the 1930s." Evidently he was concluding that our nation had crossed over into secularism during the 1930s. The national preoccupation with World War II in the 1940s and its aftermath certainly contributed to the establishing of government secularism as the most influential force in America today.

Actually, our move from the Judeo-Christian foundation of this country to the values of our current secularist state did not take place overnight. Similarly, the resultant death of our national conscience cannot be traced to a single event.

Some would make a case that the overturning of Prohibition laws against alcohol consumption was the first severe blow dealt to the American conscience. During Prohibition, the media magnified the role of gangsters and alcohol smuggling; even to this day they look on Prohibition as a mistake. In reality, however, far more deaths result each year from alcohol-crazed motorists than were ever committed by all the gangsters of Prohibition days. And those figures do not take into account the broken homes and hearts, the battered wives and children, and the crimes associated with alcohol. Despite the consequences of alcoholism, prime-time television advertising continues to present alcohol as a necessary ingredient for an adventuresome, fulfilling life. To many, however, alcohol shimmers in a cup of death.

One significant event that devastated our nation's morals was the enactment of the welfare state under the administration of President Franklin Roosevelt. The Second World War also had a detrimental effect on the moral values of our country. Infidelity abounded, and many GIs were given sex education talks by medical officers who seemed to have given up on teaching abstinence and gave in to education on condom use and disease control. With more than 15 million men away from wives and families, a wave of prostitution and promiscuity hit the military, at home and overseas.

A strong case could be made that Franklin D. Roosevelt's eight appointees to the U.S. Supreme Court changed the moral values of this country. One of these judges, Felix Frankfurter, a liberal Harvard law school professor, later bragged that he brought more people into the administration than any other individual. He was the first ACLU member to be placed on the court. These eight judges—some of whom were atheists—successfully changed the judicial process from interpreting the Constitution at face value to interpreting it in a way that, in effect, changed the laws to reflect more secularist views.

The 1948 *Everson v. Board of Education* decision was the first instance of Supreme Court violation of the First Amendment. Few Protestants understood that the decision, which forbade Catholic school children to ride to their Catholic schools on public school buses, was the first in a series of moves to secularize the country by distorting the First Amendment. This was the ACLU's first Supreme Court success, and it ushered in a relentless trail of victories that have radically affected our laws, customs, and national conscience, all in the name of freedom.

As David Barton has said, the 1962 landmark Supreme Court decision in *Engel v. Vitale* was a watershed separating an era of predominantly moral values from a laissez-faire, any-thing-goes era of relativism. By outlawing formal prayer from our nation's schools, the court opened the floodgates for educators to replace all Christian values with secular standards. Some overzealous educators have interrupted little children who, with bowed heads, were thanking God for their food in the school lunchroom and warned them against saying grace in the schools because it was "unconstitutional." It isn't, of course, but in the hands of secularists, the First Amendment of the Constitution becomes an intimidating club with which to drive any respect for God from our schools.

As Barton has pointed out, in 1962, the same year in which the Supreme Court expelled the acknowledgment of God from the schoolhouse, academic performance began its swift and consistent decline. Some estimate that a high school graduate today may not be able to read as well as an eighth grader of fifty years ago. Some, in fact, cannot read at all. Indeed, SAT scores have dropped from an average of 975 in 1960 to 899 in 1992—nearly 80 points—despite the fact that educational spending increased by more than 100 percent in that period.[4]

Pro-lifers would argue that it was the *Roe v. Wade* decision of 1973 that killed the American conscience. It would be hard to argue that legalized abortion did not contribute to our nation's loss of respect for the value of a human life. We can now add another chapter to the abortion story: the strange discriminatory decision of the Supreme Court applying RICO to those who peacefully protest before abortion clinics.

Examples are endless, but the point is clear. Using the engines of government, media, education, and the entertainment industry, secularists have had a field day assaulting the conscience of America.

THE CHURCH USED TO SPEAK AS AMERICA'S CONSCIENCE

To separate church and state is not to separate God and state. A state that refuses to acknowledge its subordination to God is on a collision course with the Lord of history.—R. C. Sproul[5]

For the first 320 years of this nation (from 1620 to 1940), churches provided the conscience of America. While individual congregations may have held different doctrinal viewpoints, they adhered to a common belief in God as the supreme Creator. He was believed to be the lawgiver of the Ten Commandments, which was held to be the standard for civil and personal morality.

Colonists overwhelmingly agreed on the new country's laws; they were a reflection of our religious beliefs. Most states had laws against murder, of course, but also against immorality, prostitution, and sodomy. (Some states still have laws on their books against sodomy.) There was a basic unity of belief for individual, family, and public behavior. Divorced people had a difficult time being elected to any public office. How things have changed!

By electing people from their midst to run for public office—from the president to the county supervisor—citizens were able to enjoy a Christian consensus in public life, as well as in personal and religious life. Because of their reverential fear of God, judges who were appointed for life sought to rule with equity. They understood that one day they, too, would stand before a judge—the judge of all the earth. Judges, like politicians, placed their hands on the Bible when they were sworn in. To this day, the U.S. Supreme Court is called to session by a marshal who announces, "God save this court."

Churches felt comfortable calling government leaders to task when they passed legislation or transacted government business in any manner that degraded the moral standard that was acceptable public policy. Even to this day, the Catholic Council of Bishops, which to one degree or another represents 52 million Americans, sends their annual encyclical to political leaders to help guide their decisions affecting public policy.

But it is obvious from the disregard our politicians have for the efforts of religious people that the majority of our nation's leaders care little about the moral condition of the nation.

THE ANTISLAVERY MOVEMENT WAS FUELED BY THE CHURCHES

While many other political and economic factors contributed to it, there may never have been an American Civil War without the abolitionist movement, which was made up of clergy and church people who found slavery to be morally wrong and contrary to biblical values.

Harriet Beecher Stowe's best-seller, *Uncle Tom's Cabin,* had a profound effect on the conscience of the northern states, stirring them to work tirelessly for the freeing of the slaves. Mrs. Stowe was the daughter of one of the most famous preachers in New England, William Ward Beecher.

Ministers' sermons were regularly punctuated with anti-slavery rhetoric. Whole denominations took an abolitionist position as they alarmed the conscience of the nation about what was, at that time, our greatest national sin.

CHURCHES IN THE CIVIL RIGHTS MOVEMENT

One hundred years after the United States made slavery illegal, many blacks still did not experience true freedom and equality. The Reverend Martin Luther King, a Baptist minister, led the civil rights movement of white and black citizens, most of whom were churchgoing people. They marched, demonstrated, and raised our nation's conscious-ness to a feverish pitch. Because they worked to instruct the nation about an immoral wrong, civil rights legislation

100

was passed to protect the rights of all American citizens regardless of race.

Tim remembers that when he served in the air force in 1944 and 1945, some bases had black servicemen assigned to permanent kitchen duties. On some bases German prisoners of war handled kitchen work; on other bases, black soldiers were routinely assigned to the tasks, but such moral and social injustice is no longer possible in our military. Today a black soldier can achieve any rank and duty to which his talents, training, and hard work entitle him.

Recently, Colin Powell, a four-star general, retired after thirty years of service. He served for more than five years as the chief of staff, a role in which he distinguished himself as a capable leader. Before the civil rights movement, he would never have been given that opportunity.

The civil rights movement succeeded in part because it was led by many church people. To this day, many of the civil rights leaders are or were ministers, and its best supporters still are church people.

AMERICA OWES HER LIFE TO HER CHURCHES

We have already seen the tremendous debt this country owes to God-fearing people, for our country was founded for religious freedom. In the early days of our country, most people did not believe a person could be trusted to hold public office unless he believed in a higher power to whom he would one day give an account for his actions.

In colonial America preachers were the most influential of citizens, the best educated of the people, and often the principle source of news for the citizenry.

Pastors, preachers, priests, and rabbis rarely hesitated to take politicians, educators, journalists, and newspaper editors to task for breaking with traditional moral values. They felt it was their duty to speak out on moral issues that influenced the family and the moral tone of their community. Church members did not consider that their religious leaders were "getting political" when they pointed out the errors of those who took positions contrary to biblical moral standards.

Unfortunately, when the moral war broke out for the cultural soul of America, fewer people took their relationship to the church seriously, and the heavy artillery of communication lay in the hands of secular people. The entertainment industry could get its amoral message to the average American home, but the religious leaders' message was either filtered or excluded. By the 1970s and 1980s, it was regularly ignored or distorted. And now the media has learned to intimidate religious leaders into near silence by accusing them of being "political." That, of course, is foolish. Their efforts have silenced the churches; meanwhile the silence continues to quiet the conscience of our nation.

America has been known around the world as a nation to be admired for her morality. She has been the land of opportunity because of the freedom and safety provided by her moral values, which were reflected in our nation's laws and public policy. The churches, or the religious people, were for centuries the conscience of the nation.

Today the churches have lost most of their influence as they have piously or passively withdrawn from the public arena. It is estimated that 38 percent or more of the population professes a "born-again experience with Jesus

Christ." It is doubtful that 10 or 12 percent of our elected public and government officials make that claim—and both our laws and our public policy reflect that deficiency. For we have spurned the Judeo-Christian ethics of our fathers and become an amoral country. Our national conscience has been seared. The moral failures of some so-called Christian leaders caused some to hold all Christianity up for ridicule, weakening the voice of Christians. But the biggest problem, for the most part, has been the silence of our churches.

What has happened to the churches and the godly influence they once had? During the sixties the church greatly influenced the civil rights movement. Where is the church of the nineties? A *USA Today*/CNN/Gallup poll taken in March 1994 found that 69 percent of those polled said that religion as a whole is losing its influence on U.S. life. Only 56 percent felt that way in a 1974 Gallup poll. Yet the recent poll finds that 70 percent belong to a church or synagogue and 66 percent attend services at least once a month.[6]

If church membership and attendance has remained stable for the last ten or fifteen years, why, then, has the influence of religion diminished? It certainly seems obvious that America is in desperate need of a spiritual awakening today.

Will the church sit back idly while our nation euthanizes our already-seared national conscience? Or will she rise up and make a moral difference by the way she votes and participates in bringing, through her influence, moral changes in her communities? The answer to that question will determine whether or not America is a secular country or "one nation under God" during the twenty-first century.

WHAT CAN WE DO?

1. Encourage fellow Christians to vocalize their concerns. Christians have not only a responsibility to obey civil laws but a responsibility to participate in government by voting our conscience and encouraging others to do the same.

2. Encourage morally sound leaders. Often Christians criticize their lawmakers for the way they vote in Congress. Yet these same Christians remain silent when it comes time to write, call, vote for, and support these elected leaders when crucial votes come up. When a congressman stands up on the floor of the House or the Senate, waving several thousand letters from his constituency, he, and sometimes his colleagues, is given the courage to act on and speak his convictions. Positive encouragement has much more influence than nasty, negative criticism.

3. Set the moral example in your own community. None of us Christians have a right to expect that our church, our community, or our nation will ever rise to moral heights we ourselves do not attain.

4. Pray for our leaders. The apostle Paul in several of his epistles called on Christians to pray for those in authority. We should never criticize a leader for whom we have not prayed or sought to influence.

5. Encourage potential leaders to run for public office, and then back them with prayer and activities that will help them win. School boards, city councils, state offices, federal offices, etc., can all be within reach if Christians would become involved in either running for office or aiding a fellow Christian who is running.

our conscience neglected:

5

This country would be much better off if our babies
were born into two-parent families.
PRESIDENT BILL CLINTON[1]

In May 1992 Vice President Dan Quayle gave a speech on family values. He raised typical themes, including the breakdown of the American family and the need for a concerted effort to strengthen this threatened institution. Attributing social anarchy to family breakdown, the vice president stated that if we don't succeed in "restoring basic values, any attempt to fix what's broken will fail. . . . When families fail, society fails. The anarchy and lack of structure in our inner cities are testament to how quickly civilization falls apart when the family foundation cracks."

Then the vice president made a comment the media would never let him forget. Despite the accuracy of his comment, the media took him to task for the following words as though he had committed a horrible crime:

> *It doesn't help matters when prime time TV has Murphy Brown—a character who supposedly epitomized today's intelligent, highly paid, professional woman—mocking the importance of fathers by bearing a child alone, and calling it just another "lifestyle choice."*[2]

To the surprise of few, the media/entertainment pundits found the vice president's comments anachronistic and inaccurate. Their reaction was a perfect example of what film critic Michael Medved refers to as the media/entertainment industry's "'circling the wagons' mentality."[3] The truth undoubtedly stung, and they weren't about to let a painful comment go by unpunished. In unison they cried out against the vice president's preference for two-parent families, as if single-parent families were equally successful and worthy of praise.

It certainly doesn't take the current experts' consent to confirm the age-old truth that a child develops best when loved and nurtured by his father *and* mother in the same home! Common sense makes that fact quite clear. Nevertheless, after the brouhaha about Quayle's remarks, magazines and newspapers, such as the *Atlantic Monthly, The Washington Post,* and *USA Today,* published lengthy articles detailing the rise in divorce in our nation and its painful toll on children.

Atlantic Monthly magazine devoted the cover of its April 1993 issue to the story:

> *Dan Quayle Was Right. After decades of public dispute about so-called family diversity, the evidence from social-science research is coming in: The dissolution of two-parent families . . . is harmful to many children, and dramatically undermines our society.*[4]

Why do we need experts to verify what we used to know intuitively? In our great learning, we tend to become so foolish that we actually begin to question eternal verities. Former vice president Dan Quayle was right: Families were designed to have two parents—a mother and a father—nurturing their children.

Dan Quayle had little success promoting the concept of family values while vice president. In fact, he was ridiculed for his promotion of two-parent families, as though the notion were passé. But in time, even his political opponents publicly conceded that he was right. President Clinton himself, after taking office, acknowledged that former vice president Quayle had raised several good points in his famous "Murphy Brown" speech. The president also acknowledged that two-parent families provide the best environment for children, and such families will ultimately strengthen our country.

After quoting facts relating to the disastrous effects of

divorce on children and on society as a whole—facts such as the threefold increase in teen suicide and the great likelihood of poverty for children in single-parent homes—the *Atlantic Monthly* article closed with these observations:

> *Over the past two and a half decades Americans have been conducting what is tantamount to a vast natural experiment in family life. . . . The results of the experiment are coming in, and they are clear. . . . This is the first generation in the nation's history to do worse psychologically, socially, and economically than its parents. Most poignantly, in survey after survey the children of broken families confess deep longings for an intact family.*[5]

Of course Dan Quayle was right. But was the "family experiment" necessary? Didn't we know that the results would point to the wisdom of God's commandments regarding family ties? Doubting the eternal, man turned to his own ways. Entertaining the vain thought that he could do whatever he wanted with impunity and with no regard for natural consequences, man only demonstrated his propensity for foolishness. When they admit Quayle was right about family values, they're really admitting that God's ways are right.

The Fruits of Weak Families

In recent days our nation has been forced to confront the fact that the decline of traditional family values has directly contributed to unprecedented illegitimacy, "absentee fathers," and escalating rates of crime, violence, and welfare dependency. Family patterns are cyclic. When a boy has no father or stable role model, or if his father is in prison or a drug dealer, it is almost inevitable that he will grow up with a distorted view of manhood. He repeats what he sees, and the cycle is perpetuated.

Between 1983 and 1992 the number of *minors* arrested for murder in the United States increased 128 percent, while the number of *adults* arrested for the same crime rose only by 8.6 percent.[6] These statistics reveal that our society is becoming more murderous, but more specifically, they show us that this problem is exacerbated among minors. Experts cite child abuse, neglect, and family breakdown as some of the primary contributors to the "plague of violence by young criminals today."[7]

There is no need to describe the specific crimes our children are committing, but we can assure you they are senseless, brutal acts that seem to be the work of psychopaths. "Unattached," psychopathic children are one result of the pathetic state of the family in America today. Dr. Ken Magid, an expert on psychopathic children who have never developed a conscience, writes:

We are in the midst of a bonding crisis. Children are becoming unattached across the nation. In your hometown. On your block. In the house next door. Perhaps, in your own home.

Factors are at play that, for the first time in this history of this country, are interfering with the basic bonding needs of America's infants. Society is in the midst of a profound demographic revolution. In the way that it affects the lives of our children this revolution is as significant as the industrial revolution that changed the course of history at the turn of the century. . . . Without suitable answers, these problems could result in a national attachment crisis, thus putting a future generation at high risk.[8]

Our children do not feel valued or loved by parents because they spend too little time with them. Fathers are all but nonexistent in too many families. Democratic Senator Patrick Moynihan has been a welcome spokesman against the dangers of the escalating illegitimacy among the black population. As he well stated, "Either there is a rebirth of moral responsibility in this area, or we are on the way to ruin."[9]

Not only are fathers absent, but mothers are spending less and less time with their children, too. For years the feminist movement's agenda has sought more help with child care so that women could be free to seek careers on their own without the encumbrance of rearing their children:

Feminism is demanding universal day care as a means of social parenting. "No woman should be authorized to stay at home and raise her children," said the late French feminist Simone de Beauvoir. "Women should not have the choice, precisely because if there is such a choice, too many women will make that one." As a socialist, Simone de Beauvoir believed that children are the property of the state, and it is therefore the government's duty to take care of them.[10]

Now the truth is coming forth. A study done by the Carnegie Corporation, a New York foundation, found evidence that the feminists were wrong:

A task force of leading business executives, medical experts and childhood specialists warned yesterday that as many as half of the twelve million American children under age three face risks that could jeopardize their futures. . . . Demographic and social changes . . . have left many of these youngest children in poverty, in single-parent homes, victimized physically by adults and in low-quality child care.

Our nation's children under the age of three and their families are in trouble, and their plight worsens every day.[11]

The Carnegie Corporation recommended more federal funding for child care and parenting education. "Clear throughout the task force meetings was concern about the quality of child care in the U.S.," the report states. "When children don't form strong attachments in their first twelve to eighteen months, they risk having troubles later—causing problems in school and failure to form strong human relationships."[12]

Are more government programs the solution to the breakdown of the family in America? Or does the answer lie in listening to our conscience, that neglected voice that tells us that families are important, that children need their mother and father, and that children are to be prized and loved and taught the principles of God's Word, for those truths are the way of life.

Even government commissions are acknowledging the devastation wrought by the decomposition of the American family. In the final report of the National Commission on Children, *Beyond Rhetoric: A New American Agenda for Children and Families,* we read:

When parents divorce or fail to marry, children are often the victims. Children who live with only one parent, usually their mothers, are six times more likely to be poor as children who live with both parents. They also suffer more emotional, behavioral, and intellectual problems. They are at greater risk of dropping out of school, alcohol and drug use, adolescent pregnancy and childbearing, juvenile delinquency, mental illness, and suicide.

The distress many children in single-parent families face undoubtedly stems from the fact that one parent is struggling to do the job of two. Single parents are often under excessive stress; they have too much to do, and they feel socially isolated. Family stress, from whatever source, reduces parents' capacity for nurturing and increases the likelihood of abuse and neglect. The routines of family life are often disrupted and disorganized. Children's need for coherence, structure, and predictability are undermined in families where parents are overwhelmed by their own struggle for emotional and financial survival. (p. 66)

Divorce devastates, and the lifelong effects of wide-scale illegitimacy and parental abandonment lead to tragic and far-reaching consequences on individuals and society as a whole.

We know America cannot long survive without strong families. The sexual permissiveness and cavalier view of the traditional family, adopted by our culture, spell disaster for our nation. We can no longer depend on government and media to promote the values we embrace, for the secularizers in government do not hold our beliefs. They have neglected

112

the voice of our national conscience and ignored the traditional family values that once made America strong.

THE NEW VIEW OF FAMILY

America's families are not only threatened from problems within the family; a relatively new external threat on the social horizon is the effort to replace the traditional notion of family—father, mother, and children—with a vague, all-encompassing definition.

In the search for ever new and different ways of perceiving life and its relationships, those with a progressive bent have promoted a concept of family that includes any group of people who join together in a wide variety of circumstances. In a very loose sense, family might mean the people you find yourself sitting next to on the bus as you ride to work.

Family, in the new sense, does not depend on a father and a mother; nor does it imply being related by blood or the covenant of marriage. In other words, anyone with whom you associate yourself could be deemed "your family." Even lesbians and homosexuals are considering their relationships *family* and are working hard to make sure the rest of society does the same.

An increasing number of Americans define *family* as "any group of people who act like family" (show love and commitment). Needless to say, under this nondescript definition, family is whatever you say it is. For many, family is merely a structure you adopt or restructure according to your needs and desires. Do you feel "love and commitment" toward someone? Then, according to progressives, those for whom you have such feelings are your "family." Should such emotions go away, you would be free to do the same, presumably to find a new "flexible family." Maintaining your personal autonomy, you do not have to commit yourself to your "family" beyond the time frame you desire.

Homosexuals are using the law as a tool to transform society's view of the family because they realize they cannot bring about the radical change they seek by any other means. They are seeking to win their battles in the courts rather than through the ballot box.

Although homosexuals and lesbians are pushing for acceptance in society, the lesbians are especially aggressive in their agenda. They have several "advantages" over their male counterparts. Unlike homosexuals, lesbians are not at high risk to contract AIDS. In addition, they are able to bear children and thus "multiply" (often through artificial insemination). Homosexual males depend on adoption for gaining children.

A large number of the major cities in the United States— New York, Atlanta, San Francisco, and Washington, D.C., to name a few—have laws recognizing homosexual "domestic partnerships." Washington, D.C.'s "Domestic Partner" law allows any district government employee to designate a "domestic partner" and obtain health insurance for that person. This is a major step toward homosexual marriages, thus further eroding God's design for the family.

Some smaller cities are following suit. In Cambridge, Massachusetts, homosexual couples can now be legally recognized as domestic partners with the privileges of marriage. The councilwoman sponsoring that legal change stated, "I feel these relationships act like families. It's important that we support them. Let's support love and commitment where it is."[13]

The wave of change hasn't stopped with domestic partnerships: In a number of places, including Washington, D.C., homosexuals are permitted to adopt children, thus furthering the concept of homosexual families. In the state of Washington, officials passed over six heterosexual couples in order to grant the adoption of a child to two homosexual men. The biological mother of the adopted child is now seeking to regain custody of her four-year-old son after learning that the state's foster care authorities had placed him in the care of these two men. Megan Lucas had given up her parental rights under the assumption that the boy would be placed with a traditional family. "This isn't what I want for my son," Lucas told the *Bellington Herald.* "I can imagine him going to school and saying this is my father, and my father."[14]

GOVERNMENT OFTEN APPEARS TO BE ANTIFAMILY

It would be nice to think that government would always be a friend of the family, but certain rulings cause some of us to doubt it. A number of laws passed today unquestionably reflect values that are antifamily. Consider that Congress granted Planned Parenthood—the organization that has been favorable to abortion and questionable sex education in this country—funds to further their causes, with or without parental consent. Consider also that government funds are providing condoms and counseling about "safe" sexual activity to minors—again often without seeking parental consent.

We've heard horrible stories about children snatched from their family because some government social worker didn't like the way the parents disciplined their children, or because unsubstantiated accusations were brought against parents for forbidding their teens to attend a dance or for insisting they go to church with them.

Last summer a couple from our former pastorate told Tim how four of their children were taken by force from their home because a counselor extracted a statement from their five-year-old that falsely accused her father of molestation. It took eight months and thousands of dollars in lawyers' fees to get their children back. During those eight months the children—one was only three years old—were bounced around from one foster home to another. By the time the youngest was returned to her parents, she was emotionally devastated.

CHRISTIAN EXAMPLE

The salt of society—the Christian influence—has lost much of its flavor. Consequently, society no longer has a model of God's standards and his prescriptions. As Fran Sciacca writes in his excellent book *Generation at Risk,* "The disintegration of the Christian home is the result of a diminishing sense of commitment to the God of the Bible and an increasing commitment to our own judgments in matters of truth and morality."[15]

Homosexuals are increasingly committed to their lifestyle, so why aren't we? If we live according to our own judgment, we will ultimately be judged by God. We must not be deceived, God is not mocked. We will reap what we've sown (see Gal. 6:7).

America has been deceived. Government programs to promote day care, health care, and domestic partnerships will not mend our broken families. What will work? Not long ago Bev read a column by William Raspberry about Robert L. Woodson, president of the National Center for Neighborhood Enterprise. Raspberry told of a discussion he had had with Woodson about his twenty years of studying *successful* American social programs. He had discovered a common thread among them: *spirituality.* "I'm not saying spiritually based programs always work," said Woodson, "only that the successful programs almost always have a spiritual base. . . . I do know that the hunger I sense in America is not a hunger for things, but a search for meaning."[16]

Bryce Christensen, editor of *The Family in America,* a publication of the Rockford Institute Center on the Family in America, accurately assesses our national problem, drawing a strong biblical conclusion:

> *The erosion of religious faith, the rise of commercial hedonism, and other cultural trends weakening marriage lie beyond the direct control of government leaders in a free republic. . . . Only through an elevated spiritual vision can Americans transcend the modern notion of wedlock as simply a working contract between two individuals and so restore the older understanding of marriage as a divinely ordained union within which husband and wife become truly "one flesh" (Gen. 2:24; Matt. 19:5).[17]*

What We Can Do

We cannot continue to neglect our national conscience in the area of our families. Just as a conscience is a safe guide only when God is the guide of the conscience, our families will be safe and strong only when they follow the biblical patterns of marriage and child rearing that have been proven successful through generations.

1. We must begin by doing all we can to strengthen our own families. Children learn first from the home example and then from the teaching of the church. A church that doesn't speak out against casual attitudes toward divorce and remarriage has no voice in the community when it speaks against single-parent families.

2. We must work to provide alternatives to abortion for young unwed expectant mothers.

3. We must make prayer for the government a priority, especially as rulings are made that appear more favorable to nontraditional family values than to the traditional Judeo-Christian moral values.

our conscience denied:

6

*In a democratic society like ours, relief must come through an aroused
popular conscience that sears the conscience of the people's representatives.*
BAKER V. CARR[1]

*Quite often when a man thinks his mind is getting broader,
it is only his conscience stretching.*
ANONYMOUS[2]

In his Gettysburg Address, Abraham Lincoln referred to
this republic as a government "of the people, by the people,
for the people." Those words may have been true in his day,
but today our government is more and more influenced by a
more liberal ruling class.

Government was instituted by God to promote justice and

119

morality, but throughout history mankind has used government to abuse the governed. Fallen men and women naturally tend to corrupt whatever they become involved with. Frequently, those who have the least desire to govern do the best job, while the power-hungry and unscrupulous manage the power of leadership worst. Very few kings, dictators, or presidents have not been corrupted by the awesome power of government leadership. As Lord Acton correctly observed, "Power tends to corrupt and absolute power corrupts absolutely."[3]

It is interesting to explore the differences between man's view of government and God's. The second chapter of the book of Daniel describes the vision of King Nebuchadnezzar in which he saw symbolized the four future world governments. The king saw them as a beautiful image with a head of gold, the chest and arms of silver, the belly and thighs of bronze, the legs of iron, and the feet of mixed iron and clay.

Historically, these four governments were the Babylonians of Daniel's day, who were replaced by the Medo-Persian Empire, who were replaced by the Greeks and followed by the iron legs of Rome that divided into two divisions, east and west. Today we seem to be living in the most unstable of all governments, iron mixed with clay, which scholars liken to democracy.

NEW WORLD ORDER

The ultimate dream of many of the world's leaders is that all who govern be elected by their countrymen and cooperate with the United Nations in the "New World Order." They entertain the hope that U.N. control of the world will assure peace on the planet. Granted, in a day of nuclear bombs and terrorists, virtually everyone wants peace. Unfortunately, however, according to the Bible and the record of history, mankind is incapable of sustaining it.

The establishment of an orderly society is the closest we can come to social peace. Such orderly societies come at a great price, for they are achieved through the suppression of liberty in dictatorial regimes. Those who control most of the Western countries of the world are using the threat of a nuclear war to impose their plans for a "New World Order" whether we want it or not. They believe a worldwide system of government is inevitable, and they may be right. Prophecy certainly indicates a one-world government is to come.

Of course God's prophecy to Daniel has been proven in the light of history. We have had only four worldwide governments, and they have all caused immense human suffering, despite the degree of education and literacy of those in authority. While the twentieth century is unprecedented in terms of universal knowledge and learning, it has also been the most barbaric in terms of human suffering—almost all of which has been caused by despotic governments.

AMERICA, THE BENEVOLENT

Few historians are eager to point out that America, the nation founded on more biblical principles than any other, has had one of the most humanitarian governments in the history of mankind. Few nations have done as much to rescue whole regions of the world from would-be dictators as America has on at least two occasions. After conquering our enemies in World Wars I and II, we signed peace treaties with them, financed their economic reconstruction, and occupied them peacefully until they were back on their feet again. Today they are our greatest business competitors on the world market, and they enjoy unusual freedom.

No country in recent history, perhaps in all history, has been so benevolent. The 350 million souls in Europe, the hundreds of millions in the Philippines, Japan, Korea, and other countries in Asia enjoy freedom today because the United States has "policed" would-be tyrants for the past half century. That benevolence has not come without a price, for the money we have spent on lend-lease plus providing their national defense has cost the American taxpayer billions of dollars.

Credit largely belongs to the Judeo-Christian roots of our country, which had such a dominant humanitarian influence on our nation that government policy was affected. Those policies were established when our nation was known as a Christian nation. Most evangelical Christians would prefer to say that our country was "Christianized," that is, the influence of our Christian founding fathers and the churches of this nation resulted in the building of hospitals, orphanages, schools, and colleges. Benevolent practices were common at home and abroad, and they were a sign of how deeply Christians had influenced this country.

In one sense the pre–World War II era of American history was "Christian" because the United States was heavily influenced by Christians. But as the secular influences on the media and education began to have their effect, largely excluding all Christian thought, our status as a "Christian" nation has gradually changed. This change accounts for much of the breakdown in the family, and marriage, and our citizenry's transformation into self-centered, greedy, selfish, even barbaric individuals.

Even though Alexis de Tocqueville was but a visitor to our land, he understood America because he had gone to our churches. In 1848 he knew that the Christian influence on America was enormous. In those days our nation recognized and spoke freely of its moral conscience. Moral absolutes were evident in our laws, education, and government policy. Virtually all Americans accepted them, with the obvious exception of a handful of atheistic socialists who were the forerunners of today's secular humanists, whose influence was felt for many years to come.

THE GREATEST FEAR OF OUR FOUNDING FATHERS

The fifty-five men who gathered in Philadelphia in 1787 had one overriding fear—that the thirteen colonies they represented would lose their freedom by the creation of a powerful federal government. This was of special concern to the small states, which were afraid of being overridden by the influence of the large states like New York and Virginia. *The Federalist Papers* were an attempt by Madison, Jay, and Hamilton to assure the people we would not end up with what we now have: a strong federal government that grows stronger by the day.

Our Constitution states, the purpose of the United States' federal government was to "form a more perfect Union, establish Justice, insure domestic Tranquility, provide for the common defense, promote the general Welfare [not welfare as we know it today], and secure the Blessings of Liberty."

Period. Gradually, however, government—federal, state, and local—has become the largest employer in the country—employing 18.6 million people, which, according to the Institute for Policy Innovation, is a greater number than are employed by the entire manufacturing sector.

Obviously, with a crime rate of 23,000 deaths per year and streets so unsafe our people are afraid to venture out after dark, the government is not doing a good job of providing "domestic Tranquility." It is instead involved with so many other things (education, ecology, and labor relations, just to name a few) that it is neglecting the civil safety of our citizens, a primary constitutional assignment.

BIG GOVERNMENT VERSUS LITTLE GOVERNMENT

One basic difference between conservatives and liberals is the size of their government. Real conservatives agree with Thomas Jefferson: "That government is best which governs least." On the other hand, liberals have a running romance with government. To them, government that controls all of life is best.

Socialism is a perfect example of the liberal view of government. Of course we don't call it "socialism" in this country—we call it "government-planned economy," or "government entitlements," or "government subsidies."

Our Declaration of Independence spoke of unalienable *rights* to life, liberty, and the pursuit of happiness, which are upheld by our Constitution. While government is not responsible to *provide* life, liberty, and happiness, it is to promote such ideals and keep us safe. Under the protection and blessing of such a government, citizens have the freedom to go out and work for happiness. Conservatives believe that if one is too lazy to get an education in order to get a job, the government shouldn't take care of that person.

SOCIALIZED MEDICINE

Present-day attempts to pass a universal health program are a good example of how government could gain control over its citizens in an attempt to *help* them. This country enjoys one of the highest levels of health care in the world. While there are weaknesses, such as those who are unwilling or unable to buy health insurance, or unscrupulous companies who use loopholes to avoid paying some claims, the majority of Americans have excellent health care when they need it. At least the problems could be settled without a total revision of the system and without so much government interference.

We would hope that this move to exercise such radical government power will be defeated as people begin to see it for what it is.

Under the current proposals, which Congress will likely change somewhat, government agencies would largely set standards, fees, charges, and even determine the extent of treatment that could be given. The first proposal, which shows how cavalier liberals are with other people's freedom, will really endanger older people by limiting what will be covered in old age. Elderly people fear that Medicare can only do so much. Some even fear that through the use of "living wills," euthanasia will be enforced with or without patients' consent or knowledge, following the example of Holland:

According to the Remmelink Report, in 1990, 8 out of 100 patients in Holland died as a result of doctors deliberately giving them overdoses of pain medication, not primarily to control pain but to hasten the patient's death. In 61 percent of these cases, the intentional overdose was given without the patient's consent *[emphasis author's].*[4]

The elderly are not the only ones put at risk by the Clinton administration's "health care package." A doctor friend pointed out to us that, in the bill's present form, the option of getting a second opinion for serious diagnoses would be eliminated, as will paying extra for the doctor of your choice. One would hope that there will be enough sane heads in Congress to strike some of these rules from this piece of social legislation before it is passed into law.

But the health care plan is only one way in which liberals are trying to increasingly control aspects of our life. "Goals 2000" is another, which calls for a federal school board, a federal curriculum, federal teacher certification, and federal testing. The plan would end nearly four hundred years of locally controlled schools in this country. Such reforms do not bring the changes Americans desire and need. If 52 percent of America's Christians and other religious citizens abstain from voting in coming elections the way they did in 1992, more unwanted reforms await us.

GOVERNMENT OUT OF CONTROL
The most expensive thing in the world is government. That is why it now costs $1.5 trillion a year to feed our federal government, and yet they still operate at more than a $200-

billion-a-year deficit. All that money comes from taxpayers—you and me. While we firmly believe that this is the best country in the world, our quality of life continues to deteriorate because of too much expensive government.

It is estimated that the average family works from January 1 to May 20 just to pay its taxes! Every year we work longer and harder to pay taxes, and something is going to have to give. Maybe we'll have a tax revolution when taxpayers grow tired of subsidizing the programs of a tax-and-spend government. If they rise up on election day and vote out of office all elected officials who have voted for tax increases, it would send a message to Washington! Our government is already bloated by bureaucrats and superfluous programs. Changes in the budget process could result in the cutting of many unnecessary personnel and programs—the same way a business has to cut whenever it is faced with deficits.

Government authority often provides unscrupulous people the power and opportunity to coerce and persecute those with whom they disagree. At a Washington press conference recently, a homosexual activist claimed that in addition to the 128 known homosexuals recently appointed to the Clinton administration or to the federal court bench, more than twenty-five hundred others occupy less-visible positions. Since presidents appoint more than seven thousand people to help them "run the country," and given this present administrations openness toward homosexuals, who can say that these figures have not been underestimated? It is true, there may have been many homosexuals holding public office in the past because homosexuality was then a "closet affair." Who can say if there are any more in office today than before the closet door was opened? But at least in the past such a lifestyle was not as openly accepted as it is today.

While we were writing this book, the assistant secretary of the Department of Housing and Urban Development (HUD) Roberta Achtenberg issued a decree that fines will be levied against anyone who puts a religious symbol in telephone company ads for rentals and housing property. That is discrimination of the worst sort, but it illustrates how conscienceless secularizers use the power of government to attack those who do not favor special rights for lesbians and homosexuals.

Secularists are rapidly fulfilling the Orwellian "prophecy" of "Big Brother." He is already here, and he is your out-of-control government in action.

SECULARISM VERSUS RELIGION: THE REAL WAR

Religious factions will go on imposing their will on others unless the decent people connected to them recognize that religion has no place in public policy.—Barry M. Goldwater, speech [5]

The so-called culture war is a struggle between religion and secularism for control of the public square. These two world views project different visions of what it means to be human. Secular society has forgotten that man has a soul.—Lawrence Criner [6]

The real war in our country is not for our culture—culture is simply a casualty. The conflict is much deeper than that. Those who resist biblical principles and morals are really warring against God. This war pits the secular-minded educators, entertainers, government leaders, and media monopolizers against conservative Christians and other groups who uphold godly values.

Secularists seem intent on moral degeneracy. In the name of broad-mindedness they demand the right for pornographers, prostitutes, and homosexuals (even advocating legislation that could be interpreted to protect pedophiles) to have the freedom to do as they please without bearing the responsibility for their actions. Little do they realize that most things that "broaden the mind" also narrow the conscience.

The national war between the theories of secular humanists and biblically based beliefs involves traditional moral values, more popularly expressed as "family values." And after this war is won, the victor will determine whether we are released from all moral restraints or whether we're free to live in good conscience according to the Bible as *one nation under God.*

The secularists demand the impossible: total freedom. But nothing is free; someone must pay for what we receive in life. Our mothers suffer nine months of pregnancy and severe labor pains to give us life, and our Savior gave his life, one for all, despite the pain he endured to save us from eternal death and anguish. Physical and spiritual life may be "free" to us, but they are not without cost to the giver. Even personal freedom is not free, for it carries with it responsibility—something too often missing from today's world. We live in a world that wants freedom without responsibility.

Counterfeit freedoms bind their captives in the most oppressive prisons imaginable: addiction, obsession, selfishness, and self-indulgence. Worse still, counterfeit freedoms frequently lead to debilitating or even fatal diseases.

What is the cumulative effect of such "freedoms" on society? Fifty years of the pursuit of freedom without responsibility has produced an undisciplined, undereducated, overtaxed population. It has also created a haven for violent people who stalk our highways and walk our streets, who can best be described as moral barbarians.

Those who uphold biblical values still represent the majority of our population, but we do not have the same power of influence that secularists have. We believe most Americans desire the freedom and happiness gained in following conscience and obeying God's moral laws. We also believe we have a constitutional right to worship as we please and that government should seek to promote an environment in which we are free to walk our streets safely after dark. We believe government should give us the freedom to raise families who can enjoy the unalienable rights given to us by God and upheld by just government.

We have allowed the unbridled power of government to take away some of what we consider God-given rights. If we sit back and let them, we could wake up to find ourselves forbidden to worship God in public (just as we are already forbidden to have public prayer in many places) and our children forbidden to thank God for their food in school. Already secular influences have taken away anything religious in the public square. Though eighty years ago a cross was given to the city of La Mesa, California, lighted, and put on a hill to serve as a landmark, now it is forbidden and has been removed lest it offend some "secular" citizen.

The secularizers in government first forbade Catholics to send their children to their parochial schools on public school buses even though they, too, were taxpayers. Then they decreed that outdated textbooks were not allowed to be given to parochial schools (it was better to trash them). Then voluntary after-school Bible lessons were banned. Then prayer was forbidden in school. Now the Bible is forbidden in some schools. (Some courts have said a Christian teacher can't have his Bible visible on his own desk lest his class think he is influenced by it.) Christian clubs meeting before or after school have been forbidden by some administrators. Now prayer is routinely being disallowed before athletic events. Now morals can no longer be taught, for they spring from religious principles. Religious books are banned from public school and neighborhood libraries.

The situation grows worse. Some parents are denied their rightful role in their children's upbringing. In many states they are not permitted to intervene should their child wish to have an abortion. Parents must bear the emotional and financial responsibility if complications arise from a "botched abortion." The child's "reproductive rights" receive higher priority than a parent's right to parent children.

And we can't forget the overzealous social workers who use the power of government to forcibly take children from their home and place them in a series of temporary child care or foster home for months (or years), while the parents go to court to prove what their neighbors and relatives freely testify: "They are good parents and qualified to raise their own children." And parents are forbidden to make the decision whether or not their children will be given condoms in school. (Big Brother government—the same government that can't keep our streets safe or deliver the mail promptly—is happy to make that decision for parents.)

WE ARE LOSING OUR RIGHTS

Some courts have been forced to rule on employment mandates for churches, to determine whether they have a right to hire or retain people who do not share their religious beliefs or moral principles. For example, a church could not refuse to hire or fire an organist on the basis of that individual's homosexual behavior. It is only a matter of time before churches are forbidden to hire counselors unless they have been certified by the state.

One of the lowest blows of secularizers is found in the guidelines issued by the Equal Employment Opportunity Commission. The EEOC wants to deprive the workplace of the freedom of religious expression. Many companies across this country were founded on Christian principles. It is not uncommon for such companies to hold chapel services once a week that employees are invited to attend.

Secularizers in the EEOC want to expand Title VII of the Civil Rights Act of 1964 to include "religious or sexual harassment" in the workplace. If this wording is approved, chapel services will become expressions of "religious harassment" even though attendance is voluntary. According to the guidelines, voluntarily witnessing to a fellow employee or giving him a gospel tract would be considered harassment. Whatever happened to freedom of speech, freedom of assembly, and freedom of religion?

Those freedoms are being stolen from us in the name of

"freedom." But the phony freedom they advocate spells destruction for true liberty. Alas, we cannot look to the Supreme Court for help. One recent appointment to that body, Ruth Bader Ginsburg, is a board member of the ACLU, the very organization that has worked tirelessly for secularists who have stolen the freedoms of religious people.

We are at war! For years Christians and other religious citizens have trusted our government to preserve our freedoms. We have not asked for handouts or special rights. We just want government to do its job of promoting justice—constitutional, criminal, and so forth—and keeping foreign countries from invading our shores.

WHY WE ARE LOSING OUR RIGHTS

Dr. Bill Bennett calls ours a devalued culture. The secularizing influences in government, education, media, and entertainment have debased, polluted, and demoralized the public square. They seem to be winning because Christians aren't paying attention. When 52 percent of the eligible Christian voters didn't even go to the polls in 1992—and of those who did, 18 percent voted their "pocketbooks" instead of morals—no wonder Christians have no more say in the present government than they do. Morally committed Christians could easily have made the difference in the future of America simply by voting.

Voting does matter and so does the religious and moral character of those for whom we vote. Despite what you may have heard from the media and despite what politicians tell you, character counts!

John F. Kennedy addressed the subject of his religious

beliefs in the July 25, 1960, *Time* magazine: "I hope that no American . . . will waste his franchise and throw away his vote by voting either for me or against me solely on account of my religious affiliation. It is not relevant."[7] Contrary to President Kennedy's insistence, moral issues and moral character *are* relevant. We are at war for America's soul, conscience, and religious freedoms, but it sometimes seems that the wrong side is winning. That's why a minority of secularists in high places are more influential than the religious majority of the nation. It is our hope that events of these days and the present climate of the government will shock the church out of its complacency and into the battle for the soul and conscience of America.

Mobilizing a majority of truly religious citizens to vote only for public officials who are similarly committed to moral values will not save anyone's soul, but it will provide a climate of civic decency and religious freedom in which the gospel can be freely presented. Secularists will not rest until they have removed every acknowledgment of God from our society and subjugated religious practice to government's heavy hand.

Christians have no need to fear sharing the true gospel of Jesus Christ in a free society. What we seek is the survival of our nation's religious liberty, protected by the Constitution that established the belief that government has no authority to dictate what or how we believe but must instead leave matters of faith in the hands of its individual citizens.

The Religion of Secular Humanism

Defining secular humanism is a challenging task because it goes by multiple names, and its essential components are often disguised by its proponents. In fact, humanists depend on deception to accomplish their ultimate objective: the undoing of Christianity. A few secular humanists call themselves socialists, but because that disparaging term has negative connotations, the politically savvy shy away from it.

Some refer to secularism as liberalism. Educators like to call themselves "progressives." Only a few radicals call themselves "Marxists" anymore, and of course, "Communist" isn't even used by the former members of the Communist Party in Russia. Instead, they're known as "hard-liners," although they have not changed one ideological premise since the fall of the Soviet Union. The American media aid this confusing process by referring to former communists as "conservatives." The term really doesn't fit unless you apply it to those who are trying to "conserve" an outdated liberal agenda.

Simply stated, secular humanism is a man-centered philosophy that teaches self-sufficient man can solve the problems of humanity without reference to a personal God. Secular humanists do not usually believe in a future life, so they see no need for a savior or forgiveness of sins. Their belief in man's ability to surmount all difficulties precludes the existence or the need of divine revelation or intervention.

HISTORY REVEALS SECULARISM AT THE SMITHSONIAN INSTITUTION

Wisdom entereth not into a malicious mind, and science without conscience is but the ruin of the soul.—Francois Rabelais[8]

135

Ever since we moved to Washington, D.C., we have wondered why the Smithsonian Institution, funded by taxpayers' dollars (its budget for 1987 was $273.4 million), is so patently atheistic and evolutionary in its exhibitions. If some atheist had set out to use it as a base of propaganda in order to undermine faith in the Bible and the church, he could hardly have thought of a better scheme.

In our research we found that in 1845 U.S. Congressman Robert Dale Owen, carrying the torch of his famous socialist father, introduced a bill to establish the Smithsonian Institution.[9] Funds were initially provided through the will of an Englishman, James Smithson, who specified that the bequest be applied toward the formation of the Smithsonian Institution "for the increase and diffusion of knowledge." As noble as the objective may appear to have been, the institution has been used to propagate evolutionary, humanistic, and socialistic dogma under the guise of "science." Regrettably, secularists have been in charge of the Smithsonian Institution from the day of its inception and have spent an enormous amount of money to build an elaborate evolutionary presentation of history.

We discovered another interesting story in our research into the Smithsonian. The U.S. Geological Society, which was founded and headquartered in New Harmony, Indiana, came about after the failure of Robert Owen's socialist colony there in 1828. Many of Owen's "free thinkers" and atheists from the colony remained in the area after the colony disbanded. The study of geology was just coming into its own at that time, and these people thought it would prove to be a mighty weapon they could wield against the Christian faith.

Educator and writer Samuel Blumenfeld, who has studied this period in depth, writes:

> *Geology, in particular, was a subject that interested the Owenites, for if it could be shown beyond a shadow of a doubt that the earth was older than the Bible said it was, this would prove once and for all that the Bible was myth and not to be believed as infallible authority. This was one line of geological research and investigation that MacLure encouraged, creating a rift between those natural scientists who believed in God and those who didn't. Curiously enough, the U.S. Geological Survey was headquartered at New Harmony until 1856 when it was moved to the Smithsonian Institute in Washington.*[10]

Keep in mind, all this happened almost one hundred years before the Scopes trial that turned the study of science in public education on its head. Educators went from teaching only creation in our public schools to teaching evolution exclusively, not only in our public schools but also in the Smithsonian Institution. And while there are many interesting historical exhibits found in the Smithsonian, a visitor cannot help but notice that a secular, evolutionary viewpoint is expressed throughout.

The Smithsonian is a favorite tourist attraction in the nation's capital and has a profound effect on those who visit its many museums. In spite of the fact that there is no solid evidence of man's presence on earth more than nine thousand years ago, the Smithsonian presents evolution as fact and leaves no doubt that man's evolution without God began millions of years ago. This institution reflects the religious bias of its founders and managers in presenting the theory of evolution as fact. If these were presented in the name of religion, we might not object, but to call evolution "science" when it is accepted by faith is intellectually dishonest.

Perhaps the worst example of Smithsonian contempt for Jesus Christ is seen in its 1994 publication of a coffee-table book entitled *Smithsonian Time Lines of the Ancient World.* This expensive book ($49.95) purports to date human history from the supposed origins of life to A.D. 1500. Of course they begin with the unscientific assumption that evolution continued for millions of years despite much scientific evidence that the earth is a very young planet. After presenting the Ice Age in chapter 2, it goes to "the first modern humans, 135,000 years ago." Then in chapter 4, it talks about pre–Christopher Columbus visits to America. They use *B.C.* when referring to dates throughout the book, until they get to page 162, where it describes events from one hundred years before Christ to A.D. 1.

As Bill Belz, editor of *World* magazine's editorial page, accurately notes, "You'll never find so much as a passing reference to Jesus Christ, the Lord of the ages. The whole book is measured around him—as of course all reality is—but he doesn't get a mention."[11] That is intellectual dishonesty of the worst order, especially given the fact that Buddha's birth and life are included in the book. All legitimate history books and encyclopedias mention the historical Jesus Christ, most giving him more space in their narration of history than they do any other person who ever lived, and rightly so. In his five-volume history set, even atheist H. G. Wells was more honest than this Smithsonian book in the treatment of Jesus Christ. Wells devoted more space to Christ and Christianity than to any other person or movement.

This flagrant display of religious bigotry and discrimination in a book officially sponsored by the Smithsonian is not only intellectually and academically dishonest but also shows the lengths to which educators and evolutionary "scientists" will go to only present their view of both origins and history. Bear in mind, what is in the Smithsonian today is or soon will be in the curriculum of tomorrow's public schools. Do we really want our children's minds inundated by this kind of brainwashing in the name of education?

The one figure in all of history most hated by secularists is Jesus Christ. Some ignore him; others deny he ever lived. Some secularizers not only hate our Lord but also detest his fixed moral standards. They seem intent on doing everything they can to oppose his standards of morality.

Probably the most confusing group of secularizers are those who call themselves religious humanists. Usually religious secularists take one of two forms: Either they undertake the destruction of religion as a lifelong quest, or they hold a mystical view of God that is nothing like the true God of the Bible. Their view is more pantheistic and New Age. Their basic view is that man is the center of the universe, morals are relative, and each man must do his best.

THE RELIGIOUS WAR OF OUR TIMES

Whatever its denominational preferences, the church is a teaching vehicle that communicates the God-centered philosophy of the Bible. That philosophy, called "the wisdom of God" by the apostle Paul, is diametrically opposed to the wisdom of man or the "wisdom of the world" (1 Cor. 1:18-25)—secularism. The diagrams that follow show these two philosophies standing in opposition to each other. One is based on the writings and thinking of man; the other is based on the Bible—the revelation of God's will for man.

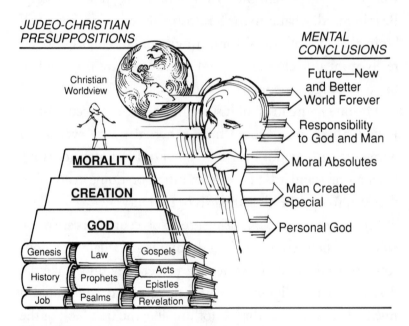

THE BELIEFS OF A GOD-CENTERED MAN

1. GOD—There is a personal God who created all things.

2. ORIGIN—God created man uniquely for himself.

3. MORALS—God has given mankind a human conscience and a moral code, the Ten Commandments. When people disobey the commandments, they feel guilty. When they obey God, their conscience approves their behavior, and they feel good about themselves.

4. PURPOSE—Man's purpose in life is to be a "servant"—first to God and then his fellowman. Man's ultimate happiness comes through serving—not being served.

5. THE WORLD—It is a temporary habitat to be used by man while he is on this earth "propagating" (teaching) the gospel and preparing for the next and eternal world that will be even better, for it will be ruled by Christ.

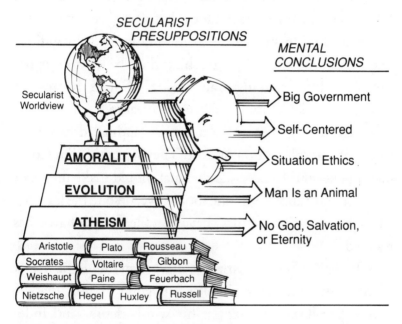

THE SECULARIST'S BASIC BELIEFS

1. GOD—Secularizers deny God's existence, despite the absence of evidence to support their atheism. The order and design of the universe clearly indicate the existence of a creator-designer. Atheists, as the apostle Paul said, who refuse to acknowledge God, have been given over to a depraved mind (Rom. 1:28). And as the psalmist said, "The fool has said in his heart, 'There is no God'" (Ps. 14:1). To believe that

this world—with all its precision and interrelated and coordinated forces—came into existence independent of a super intelligence and power is foolishness. The anti-intellectual belief in a creator-less creation is the cornerstone of the atheist's belief system.

2. ORIGIN—The theory of evolution offers the secularist an explanation for man's origin independent of God. For them, evolution replaces the divine force with natural forces. Evolution is *at best* a theory, for it has never been witnessed, and even their fossil evidence is not undisputed. Evolutionists, nevertheless, persist in teaching their beliefs to our nation's children, making one wonder if it is because it conveniently denies the existence of a creator.

3. MORALS—One of secularism's cardinal doctrines is that moral absolutes do not exist. They reject the Ten Commandments and feel every individual should make up his or her own mind about how one should live, despite the fact that wherever "situational ethics" have prevailed, social havoc has resulted.

4. PURPOSE—Secularizers believe man should be free of all restraints, that there is sufficient good in him that he should be allowed to express his selfish desires and independent spirit. But history reveals such autonomous thinking leads to moral slavery, hedonism, violence, sexual promiscuity, divorce, sexually transmitted diseases, pregnancy outside marriage, violence, and death—both physical and spiritual.

5. THE WORLD—It is a treasured resource that must be protected by a humanitarian government. Since secularists do not believe in God, they look for government to care for man from the cradle to the grave. And since they do not believe in

life after death, their unspoken creed is, "Eat, drink, and be merry, for tomorrow we die." The modern version is, "Get all the gusto you can get!" Because they do not believe in the next world or eternal life, they have neither hope nor purpose nor an understanding of their need for salvation.

NO WONDER THE BIBLE CALLS SECULARISM "FOOLISHNESS"

When you look at these two philosophies side by side, you can't help but be struck with the dark hopelessness of secularism. Secularism damns both the hearer and the teacher in this life and the one to come. Tim debated one well-known secular humanist professor who said, "When you're dead, you're dead!" What comfort can be found in learning that mankind is just another species of the animal kingdom, so we should feed our appetites while we can before we die?

In marked contrast, as a minister Tim has had the thrilling opportunity to challenge everyone who would listen with the gospel of God, namely, that God created us and wants to give us abundant, purposeful lives. Through faith in Jesus Christ, we can receive forgiveness of sins and the assurance of eternal life in heaven! We can enjoy him in this life and look forward to the beautiful eternity he is preparing for us.

The secularizers call this "foolishness," but God calls it "the wisdom of God" (1 Cor. 1:24).

Whose wisdom are we going to believe, God's or man's? The answer will affect both the way we live in this life and where we spend eternity. "For God so loved the world, that He gave His only begotten Son, that whoever believes in Him should not perish, but have eternal life" (John 3:16).

SECULARISM IS A RELIGION

Do not lose sight of the fact that secularism is every bit as much a religion as is Christianity. In fact, the Supreme Court in a 1963 decision *(School District of Abington Tp., Pa., v. Schempp)* ruled it a "religion of secularism." The ruling was based on a statement by the American Humanist Association from "Humanist Manifesto II" that appeared in *The Humanist* (vol. 33, no. 5. September/October 1973): "We affirm that moral values derive their source from human experience. Ethics is *autonomous* and *situational*, needing no theological or ideological sanction." The Court declared that belief in this dogmatic creed and its assertions concerning the nature of truth constitutes a religion.[12]

Both Christianity and secular humanism are belief systems. You cannot scientifically prove one or the other. They both have to be accepted by faith. If you can believe there is no God, that man evolved—even though that dubious theory is so unscientific that even some atheists disbelieve it—that there are no moral absolutes, and that man can live any way he wants without consequences, then you are a secularist.

Many Americans have been deceived into believing that when bad people get elected to public office, they can become good people who will do benevolent things for mankind. Impossible. Can a leopard change his spots?

Surveys show that 94 percent of Americans believe in God. In contrast, less than 6 percent are atheists. But many of the 6 percent work in education where they can influence the minds of millions of children and youth who come from God-fearing families. Gallup polls indicate that 62 percent of the population of this country believe Jesus Christ is God, and a similar number believe he is coming back to this earth in what the Bible calls "the Second Coming." But you would never see that belief reflected in media, entertainment, education, or government because that belief is foreign to most of the people who control those influential agencies in our society. From their government-granted pulpits, they communicate their religious beliefs and values—and most of that communication is at our expense!

Admittedly, there are some Christians in those influential agencies (about 12 percent of public schoolteachers profess to have been born again). But they don't have much influence, either, because of discrimination or because they are afraid to communicate their faith and its values. Occasionally we find a local media spokesperson who admits to being a Christian, but the best he or she can do is "slip in a slight testimony." Why? Because the secularizers control the public thought in this country.

We saw an illustration of that when the space shuttle blew up several years ago. That horrifying event took place in front of the cameras of the world and was beamed into thousands of school classrooms because a schoolteacher was aboard. Almost all those children and many of the adults wanted desperately to pray that day, but only teachers who were willing to break the law led their children to pray for those who were killed and for their families. The secular humanist cannot pray, for he has no loving heavenly Father to whom he can turn when all of life's dreams explode.

One secular humanist philosophy professor, whom Tim formally debated, wrote a magazine article in which he told of the death of his grandson. Standing at the child's crib, this highly educated secularist scholar said, "My son, you shall live as long as I live, for you will live in my mind." While we can feel his grief, we must point out that his view is hopeless. The hopelessness of secularism is worse in the next life than it is in this one.

If there is anything that should make us aggressive about sharing our faith, it is the contrast between the hope and joy of Christianity and the utter hopelessness and despair of secularism.

THE SECULARIZED MULTITUDES IN THE VALLEY OF DECISION

When Jesus saw the multitudes, he felt compassion for them because they were "distressed and downcast like sheep without a shepherd" (Matt. 9:36). Throughout America today, millions of people are blindly following secularist leaders. These multitudes, who basically believe in God but have never taken him or his plans for their life seriously, have been severely influenced by their secularist teachers.

They don't share the secularist view of God and life after death—they may even try to reconcile evolution and creation by adhering to "theistic evolution." Or they may avoid thinking about it altogether. Some of these victims of secularism may leave the church and adopt the social lifestyle of the world. Some even become hedonists or moral barbarians and never return. Others, if they marry, may return to the church when they begin to have children and are confronted with the responsibilities of parenthood.

One thing they almost never do is make any kind of social

contribution to their country. Since they were educated—or indoctrinated, depending on your point of view—by secularists, they usually accept liberal moral values for themselves and for society in general. When it comes to exercising the responsibilities of citizenship by voting, they either don't investigate a candidate's moral values or they say, "I don't think I should impose my moral values on others." Why not? Secularists have never hesitated to impose their relativistic "values" on the rest of us!

Our nation began with a deep sense of high moral values. It has been the influence of secularization that has changed our laws to allow such sins as abortion and gambling but has forbidden school children to pray.

Sadly, the effects of secularism couldn't have happened without the help of a lot of people who stood by and allowed it to happen. Because of the absence of Christian votes and voices, a minority of people have gained control of our most influential agencies, among them education, the media, and the entertainment industry, and now have the power to determine who gets elected to the government.

Gradually some among the secularized masses are recognizing that family values are important and that there should not be special rights allowing homosexuals to marry and adopt children. Recent appointments to high government offices of people with "progressive" views on the family are sounding an alarm to many who would prefer a culture of traditional values in which to raise their family. The present direction of liberalism in government is becoming more and more destructive to our nation's conscience and way of life.

What We Can Do

If before the next election enough Americans wake up to the fact that their votes count and that they should elect to government office only those who have a deep commitment to traditional moral values, we may yet see the social change our nation needs. Any nation that mocks the laws of God by legalizing immorality will experience God's wrath and judgment as it speeds down the road to Sodom and Gomorrah.

Maybe, just maybe, there are enough strains of moral sensibility left in the masses of America to bring about a revival in righteousness. If not, we all will discover shortly that we are on a collision course with wholesale corruption and anarchy.

At the dedication of the Focus on the Family headquarters building, Charles Colson predicted that unless our present course changes, he sees anarchy in this country in five years. If you doubt that, just look again at the Los Angeles riots. For the people who live in L.A., anarchy has already come. Such are the consequences of a national conscience that has been denied.

our conscience silenced:

7

The God-given rights of parents are not understood or are ignored by our secularist educators and by many school administrators who, in the delusion of sovereignty, act as though they, not the parents, have complete control of the education of the child.
JOHN T. MCNICHOLAS[1]

The parents have a right to say that no teacher paid by their money shall rob their children of faith in God and send them back to their homes skeptical, or infidels, or agnostics, or atheists.
WILLIAM JENNINGS BRYAN, THE SCOPES TRIAL[2]

The philosophy of the school room in one generation will be the philosophy of government in the next.
ABRAHAM LINCOLN

Abraham Lincoln was right: He who controls the education of this generation controls the public policy of the next. We cannot entrust our most prized possession—our children—to those whose mind-set is hostile toward God. Now, more than ever before, we must diligently care for and oversee the growth of the budding generation. As Alexander Pope so beautifully put it, "'Tis education forms the common mind: Just as the twig is bent, the tree's inclined."

EARLY AMERICAN EDUCATION

Despite the presence of immigrants in America holding other philosophies, education in America was basically framed on Christian beliefs during the colonial period and for more than 150 years after the founding of the United States. Prayer in the classroom was expected; creation was taught exclusively as late as 1925. The Ten Commandments were extolled in the 1930s and 1940s. Although secular humanism started pouring into the classroom during the 1960s, the religious truth about American history was taught until the 1980s despite the fact that religious morals had been abandoned long before that.

During America's first century more than a hundred colleges were founded by Christian denominations. The first college was founded in 1836, just sixteen years after the Pilgrims landed on Plymouth Rock. Reverend John Harvard founded Harvard College for the purpose of training ministers and missionaries for the next generation.

Today, however, Harvard is arguably one of the most liberal universities in the country. Its law school has turned the U.S. Constitution on its head, particularly the First Amendment.

Its effect on teacher training has secularized our once moral-ity-based public school system, turning it into one that today provides an inferior education and produces students who are hostile to traditional moral values.

THE REMNANTS OF HARVARD DIVINITY SCHOOL

One wonders what John Harvard would think if he could see what has happened over the last three and a half centuries at the university that bears his name. Harvard Divinity School no longer appears to be in the business of training theologians to understand the Holy Scriptures and preach the Word without apology. Nationally syndicated columnist Don Feder writes that the student newsletter at Harvard, the *Nave*, alerted students to the following during Palm Sunday week, 1994:

> *Instead of singing hymns, they're sitting in the lotus position, chanting "omm" at America's oldest school of theology. The* Nave's *calendar reminds students that March 20 is Spring Ohigon, "a special time to listen to the Buddha and meditate on the perfection of enlightenment."*[3]

Notice that the *Nave* did not remind students of Palm Sunday, Passover, or Easter. "The publication also lists a peace dance, meditation sessions, a Nigerian tribal drum performance, feminist symposiums, and a showing of 'Thelma and Louise.'"[4]

Bev was so overcome by the article by Don Feder that she contacted him to share this information on her radio program *Beverly LaHaye Live.* They discussed how the Reverend Mr.

Harvard had had a great vision to train biblically oriented ministers, yet today this school is helping to train the next generation of ministers and leaders by educating them with a godless doctrine. If it were not for a few strong evangelical colleges and universities in America that are training pastors, missionaries, and lay people, there would be little hope for the future of America's spiritual leadership.

The courses in a catalog from Harvard Divinity School reveal where the school stands on biblical truth:

> *At the pinnacle of the school's pantheon are feminism (goddess worship) and liberation theology (Marxism of the miter). Its catalog lists courses in Feminist Biblical Interpretation, Introduction to Feminist Theology, and Feminist Critical Theories and Radical Critiques of Religion.*[5]

Don Feder sums up the future for those who would choose to attend a liberal mainline church led by ministers with this kind of training:

> *Why go to church when you can get the same message in the pages of Ms. magazine or the collected writings of Kim Il Sung?*[6]

I would apologize to Rev. John Harvard because his vision for the spiritual future of this nation has been taken over by people who no longer honor Jesus Christ as the only Way. This could probably be said for many other schools of learning where the Bible has been replaced with feminist, secularist, and Marxist doctrine.

THE DEVELOPMENT OF A CHRISTIAN CONSCIENCE

During the first one hundred years of colonial history, there were 128 colleges founded by religious groups that taught what the late Dr. Francis Schaeffer referred to as "a Christian consensus," a Christian or biblical view of law, culture, and morality.

Many of the one-room schoolhouses that were so famous during those years were run by local ministers. Harvard, Princeton, and Yale became the headquarters for preparing schoolteachers in our growing nation. And all three of those schools were originally founded to train ministers and missionaries. Schoolteachers were, and still are, purveyors of the moral code recognized by the customs of the country.

Unfortunately, most modern teachers no longer teach the traditional values of our founding fathers but teach the secular humanistic philosophy, which is based on theories of life and religious skepticism. Is it any wonder that private Christian schools and home schooling have grown to such enormous proportions? In most cases, alternative education is parents' only solution to the secularization of our public education system.

THE NORTHWEST ORDINANCE OF 1787

The same year our founding fathers gathered in Philadelphia to write our nation's Constitution, the Continental Congress passed the Northwest Ordinance, in which we find yet another evidence of how important our founding fathers considered religion to be. In Article 3, the Congress wrote, "Religion, morality, and knowledge, being necessary to good government and the happiness of mankind,

153

schools and the means of education shall forever be encouraged."[7]

That this congressionally approved statement was made didn't guarantee that all their lofty goals came into fruition, but it shows their intentions. Those who drafted it recognized what modern educators seem to ignore: The teaching of religion is essential in producing good citizenship and moral values.

To demonstrate that such a statement reflected the popular thinking of that day, we have only to summon the testimony of President George Washington in his farewell address, delivered more than ten years later:

> *Of all the dispositions and habits which lead to political prosperity, religion and morality are indispensable supports. . . . Let us with caution indulge the supposition that morality can be maintained without religion. . . . Reason and experience both forbid us to expect that National morality can prevail in exclusion of religious principle.*[8]

NOAH WEBSTER: "AMERICA'S SCHOOLMASTER"

One of the great Christian statesmen and educators at the end of the colonial period was Noah Webster, famous for the dictionary that bears his name. He was also an active politician, a noted public servant whose faith played a prominent role in his public life. He served nine terms as a member of the Connecticut General Assembly, three in the Massachusetts legislature, and four years as a judge. In addition, he played a significant role in the ratification of the Constitution.

Noah Webster also had strong opinions about the relationship between Christianity and government:

The religion which has introduced civil liberty, is the religion of Christ and his apostles, which enjoins humility, piety, and benevolence; which acknowledges in every person a brother, or a sister, and a citizen with equal rights. This is genuine Christianity, and to this we owe our free constitutions of government.[9]

With regard to the role of the Scriptures in the founding of society, Noah Webster noted the following:

The moral principles and precepts contained in the Scriptures ought to form the basis of all our civil constitutions and laws. All the miseries and evils which men suffer from vice, crime, ambition, injustice, oppression, slavery, and war, proceed from their despising or neglecting the precepts contained in the Bible.[10]

In addition to his other accomplishments, Noah Webster authored textbooks, dictionaries, spellers, and catechisms. As David Barton has observed,

Webster recognized that education must continue to transmit the principles that gave birth to the nation. He believed that education was the guardian of true republican principles and that the success of our government depended upon the quality of our education.[11]

In Webster's own words:

In my view, the Christian religion is the most important and

one of the first things in which all children, under a free government, ought to be instructed. . . . No truth is more evident to my mind than that the Christian religion must be the basis of any government intended to secure the rights and privileges of a free people.[12]

McGUFFEY'S READERS

Another evidence of the Christian foundations in education for the first one hundred or more years following the writing of the Constitution was the popularity of McGuffey's Readers, primers that were used in virtually every school in the country. They were filled with moral values and biblical precepts and principles for building good character. William H. McGuffey was a minister of the gospel, so naturally his early readers carried with them the values and morals of the Bible. Although many considered McGuffey's Readers to be among the best tools for teaching children to read, they were taken out of use primarily because of their religious content.

HOW HUMANISM DISTORTED AMERICAN EDUCATION

One of the most disturbing stories in our history concerns the way this once great Christian nation was turned into a godless nation, the very thing its founders tried to avoid. Many think the process was brought about by a master conspiracy; some think it was because Christians over the years took too much for granted, sitting back and letting the changes come unchallenged; others believe it was orchestrated and executed by the devil himself working through intelligent, well-educated people who had in common a low regard for the God of the Bible. Some, like Horace Mann, known as "the father of public education," rejected Jesus Christ in dramatic experiences that haunted them throughout their life. Mann had also rejected the Calvinistic beliefs and traditions on which he was raised. Mann was unusual; through much of his life he maintained the moral code of his youth in his personal behavior while he introduced a philosophy to our nation's schoolchildren that would ultimately etch away the moral values others had fought to preserve.

There were others, like the British philosopher Robert Owen, "the father of socialism," who were openly hostile to religion. During the 1830s he was forced to go underground with his philosophies of education. He advocated compulsory public education with secular curriculum, teachers, and libraries.

Who would deny that Owen's scheme has succeeded? It took more than 160 years to fulfill his goal, but Robert Owen's dream has come true. Another recent manifestation of it is called "Goals 2000."

Today 45 million American schoolchildren receive a secularized education at the cost of $500 billion every year. Indeed, the education business is the second largest industry in the nation, second only to the health care industry. Our educational system is almost completely anti-Christian and antimoral, contrary to the original purpose of the founding fathers.

THE UNITARIAN-HUMANIST CONNECTION

The battle for the soul of Europe was waged largely in Switzerland between John Calvin, one of the fathers of Protestantism, and Michael Servetus, who rejected the Trinity and particularly rebelled at the concept of Jesus Christ's deity. Servetus's heretical views brought on him the wrath of both the Catholic Church and the burgeoning new Protestant movement. He was finally tried for heresy, found guilty, and burned at the stake in 1553.[13] Unfortunately, his heresy did not die with him. Instead, it was developed into early Unitarianism by his followers and spread throughout Europe, particularly among the so-called intellectuals, who rejected the God of the Bible. Calvin considered Unitarianism the most dangerous heresy in Europe. Considering the influence that the Unitarian movement in this country had on the secularism that now dominates American public education, it proved to be equally dangerous in America.

By the time Unitarianism came to Puritan Boston, the philosophy had been influenced by German rationalism, illuminism, French skepticism, the Enlightenment, and even the atheistic ideology of Hegel, the philosopher whose concepts formed the basis for much of Nietzsche's thought, marxism, communism, and Nazism. These were philosophies about mankind from which came secular humanism, the philosophy that has greatly influenced our public schools today.

THE "FRIENDS OF EDUCATION"
Although there were some atheists in this country at its founding in 1789, for the most part they had limited influence. While God-fearing people were establishing schools to train ministers and missionaries, Boston, the center of Unitarianism, became a hotbed of European-originated rationalism, skepticism, and other atheistic philosophies.

Boston was the home of Harvard College, and in fact, Massachusetts could have been regarded as the birthplace and stronghold of American education.

Samuel L. Blumenfeld is a distinguished educator who has carefully researched both public and private education in America. In his book *Is Public Education Necessary?* he writes:

> *Apart from New England, where tax-supported schools existed under state law, the United States, from 1789 to 1835, had a completely laissez-faire system of education. Although the idea of the town-supported common school had spread westward with the migration of New Englanders and was encouraged by the federal land grants, there were no compulsory attendance laws anywhere. Parents educated their children as they wished: at home with tutors, at private academies, or church schools. . . . Some states paid the tuition of poor children, enabling them to attend the private school of their choice. Virtually every large city in the country had its "free-school" societies that built and operated schools for the poor and were supported by the community's leading benefactors and philanthropists. Such schools were considered extremely worthwhile causes for philanthropy. Often these schools also received small grants from local governments in recognition of their public service.*[14]

From the earliest days in American history, parents seriously heeded the rights and responsibilities of educating their children as they pleased. Christians in this country assumed that the education of their children's minds was as much their responsibility as was their spiritual upbringing. In many cities and towns, ministers were often the first teachers. They were usually among the best-educated individuals in a community, and since they needed to supplement their income, the teaching of the children often fell to them. Men of God naturally included character-building values and religious doctrines in the lessons taught at the schoolhouse.

In the larger cities and towns, the private school enjoyed a higher academic reputation than the common school:

Freemarket forces were slowly shifting public favor from the poorly managed public school to the more efficiently managed private school. Only in Boston did the public schools receive unflagging public support despite the competition from private academies, mainly because of a special situation in that city: the growth of the Unitarian movement which strongly favored public education.[15]

Over the years, education in America began to feel more influence from those who held to views of secular humanism, the foundation of public school education today. Unitarianism, which had a lot of influence on the changes that took place, was headquartered in Boston, the very center from which compulsory education sprang.

Educator Samuel Blumenfeld, with whom many may disagree, holds the Unitarian movement as greatly responsible for the educational philosophies of our public schools today:

The takeover of Harvard in 1805 by the Unitarians is probably the most important intellectual event in American history—at least from the standpoint of education. The

circumstances that signaled the takeover were the election of
liberal theologian Henry Ware as Hollis Professor of Divinity
and the subsequent retreat of the Calvinists to a new seminary
of their own in Andover, Massachusetts. From then on Har-
vard became the Unitarian Vatican, so to speak, dispensing a
religious and secular liberalism that was to have profound
and enduring effects on the evolution of American cultural,
moral, and social values. It was, in effect, the beginning of the
long journey to the secular humanist worldview that now
dominates American culture.[16]

Harvard University may serve as a paradigm of what happened in the following years. Within eighty years of the founding of Harvard College, liberal theologians tried to gain control of this citadel of Christian teaching. For almost a hundred years the controversy raged between fundamentalists and liberals. Many of the ministers of the larger churches traveled to Europe and returned with even more liberal thinking, exercising an increasing influence upon Harvard, ultimately moving it permanently into the liberal (eventually humanist) camp.

At that time in history, Germany was a hotbed of rationalism and higher criticism. In the name of academic intellectualism, American liberals brought this so-called scholarship from Germany to Harvard, from which it was disseminated to other schools, colleges, and seminaries, ultimately affecting the liberal movement in theology and the secular movement in public education.

Robert Owen, the father of modern socialism, dreamed of the establishment of an educational system to condition the minds of future generations for socialism. After his disastrous failure to establish a successful socialist colony in New Harmony, Indiana, in 1826, he concluded in 1828 that one ingredient for socialist success was lacking: compulsory secular education. Thus, the Owenites and other humanistic forerunners launched the philosophical takeover of the public education system.

Orestes A. Brownson, a Universalist minister who joined the Owenites in the 1820s but later converted to Catholicism, revealed in his autobiography that in the late 1820s the Owenites organized as a secret society for the purpose of instituting universal public education:

> *The great object was to get rid of Christianity, and to convert our churches into halls of science. The plan was not to make open attacks on religion, although we might belabor the clergy and bring them into contempt where we could: but to establish a system of state—we said national—schools, from which all religion was to be excluded, in which nothing was to be taught but such knowledge as is verifiable by the senses, and to which all parents were to be compelled by law to send their children. . . . The first thing to be done was to get this system of schools established. For this purpose, a secret society was formed. . . . It would be worth inquiring, if there were any means of asserting how large a share this secret infidel society, with its members all through the country unsuspected by the public, and unknown to each other, yet all known to a central committee, and moved by it, have had in giving the extraordinary impulse to godless education*

*which all must have remarked since 1830, an impulse
which seems too strong for any human power now to
resist.*[17]

During the 1830s a controversy raged between the Friends
of Education (a title describing a coalition of socialists, Unitarians, atheists, educators, and others who favored tax-sup-
ported, government-controlled public schools) and those
who were committed to private schools. The former believed
it was the government's duty to educate our young; the latter
were convinced that parental responsibility came first. That
controversy rages still, although with 90 percent of the Christian parents still sending their children to public schools, it is
obvious who is winning. That could be the main reason so
many Christian young people are lost to the world before they
graduate from high school.

EDUCATION'S "FRIENDS" HAD A PLAN

Three basic goals necessary to their plan for public schools
were established:

1. Make school attendance compulsory.

2. Establish government-sponsored "free" schools. This
plan was sold to the nation on the basis that "free" would
insure education for all the poor. Ironically, according to an
1817 survey, 96 percent of the children of Boston, where this
proposal was made, were already in some school at the time,
and the other 4 percent had access to "charity schools" if their
parents so desired.[18]

3. Establish standards for teacher-training schools. At first
these were called "normal schools," like denominational sem-

inaries where ministers were indoctrinated with denominational theology and practice. In these "teacher seminaries"
future educators were taught based on secular philosophies.

After studying the history of American education, it is easy
to see why our twentieth-century schools are so antagonistic
toward God, religion, morality, and Christianity. If you don't
believe they are, just try holding a Bible class on campus. Or
ask the former principal of Wingfield High School in Jackson,
Mississippi, who was fired from his job because he gave
permission for a student to have a morning prayer in school.
Or talk to Dan Scott of Springfield, Ohio, who was relieved
of his teaching duties after students accused him of "injecting
religious views" into a class on evolution at Wright State
University.[19]

THE FATHER OF PUBLIC EDUCATION

Horace Mann is usually considered the father of public education. Actually, the present secular direction in public education was already set in motion while he was still a struggling
attorney. In Boston, the Friends of Education, led by socialist
Robert Owen, Josiah Holbrook, and others, had begun the
trend of secularism in public education.

In 1830, at one of Josiah Holbrook's lyceum meetings for
schoolteachers and educators, the delegates voted to form the
American Institute of Instruction. Holbrook's followers cam-
paigned vigorously for a state-supported school system financed by property taxes. Their campaign slogan: Crusade
against ignorance. Now, after 147 years of their relentless
secularizing of our once-superior school system, they should
perhaps change their slogan to Perpetuate Ignorance. With

the removal of the religious and moral values of Christianity from the curriculum, we now have an education system and a society that have helped produce a generation that even Barbara Walters recognized as "cultural barbarians." Thanks to their infidelity and antagonism to Christianity, many big-city classrooms are no longer safe. More than 250,000 weapons were taken to school last year, and academic progress and test scores are steadily dropping.

Horace Mann had very little success as an educator. His limited teaching experience was a two-year tutorship at Brown University in 1820 and 1821, where it is said that one day the students "hissed and hooted him out of class."[20] Horace Mann was selected for his Massachusetts post because of his connections with the board members of the Friends of Education.

As a lawyer, Mann had distinguished himself as an orator, had successfully run for public office, and was highly respected among the Unitarian elite of Boston. One of the little-known facts about his life is that at twelve years of age, he was taken by his parents to revival meetings, where he fell under deep conviction. Unlike many of his youthful associates, however, he did not receive Christ. He later wrote, "I remember the day, the hour, the place and the circumstances, as well as though the event had happened but yesterday, when in an agony of despair, I broke the spell that bound me."[21]

Following that experience, Mann constructed his own theory of Christian ethics and doctrine, which was based on a denial of a personal God, man's fallen nature, a divine Savior, and the need to be born again. Mann retained a lifelong antagonism toward Christianity and the Bible.

Most people do not think of Horace Mann as an educational prophet, but his first annual report to the Massachusetts Board of Education on January 1, 1838, contained a "prophecy" that radiated frightening overtones:

> *And what citizen of Massachusetts would not feel an ingenuous and honorable pride, if, in whatever direction he should have occasion to travel through the State, he could go upon no highway, nor towards any point of the compass, without seeing, after every interval of three or four miles, a* beautiful temple, *planned according to some tasteful model in architecture, dedicated to the noble propose of improving the rising generation, and bearing evidence, in all its outward aspects and circumstances, of fulfilling the* sacred object of its erection *[emphasis added]?*[22]

Mann was referring to the thousands of elementary and junior and senior high schools that occupy some of the most valuable land and possess the finest facilities and equipment in our nation—but propagate their anti-God, anti-Christian, antitraditional moral values and doctrines of secular humanism. Who has not seen these temples of learning "after every interval of three or four miles"? Our public schools are temples of the religion of atheistic humanism, which deifies human nature and advances a socialist worldview.

Originally our nation's schools were governed by local school boards of five or more people elected by the community. If these trustees permitted educators to initiate policies and programs that counteracted the values of the community and its homes, they could be recalled or voted out of office at the next election. We still go through the motions of such elections, but school boards have tended to give the educators of their district free rein in running the schools and choosing curriculum.

Gradually, Christians and others committed to traditional moral values are waking up to the fact that these schools, while not necessarily being Christian schools, should at least respect the beliefs of the community. As taxpayers, we should use our influence in our community schools. But even when we do gain local representation, we make a horrifying discovery. As one school board president confided to us, "We local trustees have very little control over our districts. By the time the state board of education and the federal Department of Education get through with their state and federally funded programs, we have little choice but to go along."

To Mann, who believed the Normal School to be "a new instrumentality in the advancement of the race," the linking of state power to teacher education was indeed a crowning circumstance, creating what James G. Carter had described in 1825 as a powerful "engine to sway the public sentiment, the public morals, and the public religion, more powerful than any other in the possession of government." And once a nation's teachers' colleges become the primary vehicle through which the philosophy of statism is advanced, this philosophy will very soon infect every other quarter of society, for the most potent and significant expression of statism is a state educational system. Without it, statism is impossible. With it, the state can and has become everything.[23]

167

Mann—First Federal Secretary of Education

Horace Mann moved from the Massachusetts Department of Education to become the first secretary of the Department of Education for the federal government. What he did for education in Massachusetts he ultimately duplicated for all of America:

1. Education was made compulsory and public. (This eventually drove many private schools out of business.)

2. State teachers colleges were established, indoctrinated with a "nonsectarian" philosophy of education. These American teachers sat at the feet of secular educators. Gradually our schools and libraries no longer reflected the theism of the founding fathers.

3. Control of our schools was taken from parents and local communities and given to the "state." Humanist educators seemed more interested in the indoctrination of our youth with theories of humanism than in teaching true knowledge and in the students' academic achievement.

From Mann to "Progressive Education"

Horace Mann was followed by many other secularists who built on his humanistic foundation of education. John Dewey, among others, promoted a number of controversial teaching techniques, many of which challenged moral absolutes. After him came sex education, values clarification, and a plethora of programs that have proven ineffective and destructive, which left children undereducated and parents, who would want more traditional values taught, defrauded.

One recent educational innovation is known as Outcome-Based Education (OBE). This multifaceted system is designed to indoctrinate students with "politically correct" values in order to produce desired attitudes and behaviors. Many object to the program, claiming it manipulates students in order to attain specified objectives. OBE infringes on their personal rights and undermines the role of parents.

Benjamin Bloom, the "philosophical grandfather" of OBE, states in his *Taxonomy of Educational Objectives* that students have attained the highest level of intelligence when they no longer believe in the existence of truth. Fittingly, relativism (the denial of the existence of an objective standard of right and wrong) is OBE's linchpin. Is it any wonder that our nation is experiencing a crisis of values?

Because OBE emphasizes the *affective* (feelings and emotions) and downplays the *cognitive* (facts and knowledge), under this system facts are viewed as incidental, while a readiness to change and conform is considered fundamental. Students are made to learn "higher order thinking" rather than information, concepts, and essential skills. But without a factual knowledge base, how are students to employ such thinking?

It is clear that OBE's proponents do not make the betterment of students' academic education a priority but choose instead comprehensive societal control from preschool on.

OBE is both extremely experimental and costly. Those who favor it are either unaware of its true nature and goals or are convinced that the economic dividends OBE is supposed to yield (by producing compliant workers for the twenty-first century) justify its infringement on freedom of conscience and personal liberties.

Goals 2000, the national education reform plan, is an

unprecedented federal takeover of the educational system. It not only paves the way for OBE across the nation but also creates three federal bureaucracies: the National Education Goals Panel, the National Education Standards and Improvement Council, and the National Workforce Skills Standards Board, which would further erode local autonomy. While its national goals and standards may start out as voluntary, history teaches that government plans that start out as options are swiftly transformed into mandates.

Many parents feel that the real impact of Goals 2000 on families and on education will be, to put it simply, loss of control. Local schools will lose control of curricula. In order to get federal dollars, schools must march in lockstep to national reform. And in order for children to graduate, parents will no longer have the right to pass on the values *they* feel are important to their own children. Instead, America's schoolchildren must accept the beliefs that the educators who prepare the program name as acceptable and politically correct.

The first of the national education goals established by Goals 2000 states that "all children will start school ready to learn." But what does it mean to be "ready to learn"? To these educationists, it means having proper "self-esteem" and other nebulous standards. But how does the government intend to ensure that children meet these standards?

WILL CHRISTIAN PARENTS EDUCATE THEIR YOUNG?

Public education today is disastrously deficient. Not only has it become anti-Christian, it has failed academically and brought about moral chaos and, in some schools, barbaric behavior. More than a million acts of violence take place in our public schools annually—250,000 involving weapons. Academics have suffered, with many high school graduates unemployable because they are so poorly educated.

Yet 90 percent of America's Christian families still send their children to public schools. Admittedly, 12 percent of the nation's teachers are Christians, which leaves 88 percent who teach an education based on a non-Christian worldview.

Studies show that 35 to 50 percent of our church young people leave the church by the time they graduate from high school today. While many parents and pastors wring their hands and call for prayer, they do little to provide an alternative. Parents, through their tax dollars, are paying for the moral and educational destruction of their children when only unacceptable, man-centered, relativistic philosophies are taught.

SCHOOL CHOICE—HOPE FOR RENEWAL

"School choice" or tuition vouchers are a means of breaking the steel grip now held by secularist educators on the minds of our children. When parents receive vouchers, they are able to enroll their children in the school of their choice, which levels the playing field between public schools and private schools. If legislation providing tuition vouchers is approved, most Americans who want their children to receive a solid education with traditional values could afford to take their children out of the public school and send them to a Christian school. At the same time, parents who want to send their children to public schools, where completely secular values are taught, would be free to do so.

171

One Christian mother heard about the proposed California tuition vouchers plan and talked to a neighbor about it. Her neighbor, a public school counselor, seemed unexcited about the idea of vouchers. "Why isn't it a great idea?" the Christian woman asked. "According to the California plan, education costs $5,000 a year per child. The voucher plan gives parents a voucher for $2,400 to pay for a private school education, and if the parents find a school that costs less than $2,400, they can put the remaining money in a college savings account. Meanwhile, the public school will still receive the remaining $2,600 it would have ordinarily received, but it won't have to pay for educating the child because he will no longer attend that school. Parents would have a choice about where to send their children, plus kids would have a head start on their college funds. And you folks at the school would be making money on the plan!"

"No," the counselor said, shaking her head. "I don't like it. If Congress passed tuition vouchers, everybody'd take their kids out of public school. Besides, you send your kid to a private school now, and I still want all $5,000 of your tax dollars!"

Naturally, there is a great deal of opposition to the tuition vouchers plan. The National Education Association and others make their living off the huge tax revenues now collected for public education. They admit that most parents would take their kids out of our troubled schools if given the chance. They keep holding out hope to parents that somehow some of their experimental curriculum will start to work and produce better educated, more socialized graduates—but our schools keep getting worse.

We need to pray that something is done in our nation's education system, and we need to consider what we can do as individuals for the education of our own children. It is time that the church saw the need to train up its members in God's ways, as Martin Luther, John Calvin, and the Pilgrims did. We can't expect humanistic educators to produce a generation of God-fearing children with strong moral convictions. Just hoping public school educators will be neutral and allow the views and values of parents, who pay for the system through their taxes, to be reflected in the classroom along with other views—as most parents mistakenly do—is naive. Except in rare communities that hasn't been done since the 1950s.

If we cannot trust public education to impart true knowledge and constructive information and skills to our children, we must pursue another course. One significant alternate route would be the availability of vouchers promoting school choice, but without government intrusion. Another option is home schooling, a popular practice often harassed, despite the fact that most home-schooled children are academically superior to public school graduates. It is time that our nation restored the realm of education to its rightful owners: parents and local communities.

A VICTIM OF SECULARISM

Recently we talked to a brilliant engineer, a member of the church we pastored for twenty-five years. We asked about his children, whom we knew well as they were growing up. Their daughter was married with three children and active in a

Bible-believing church. Their son had become a medical doctor but in the process had left the faith. All the while this young man was growing up, our church offered one of the finest Christian schools in the nation. But these dedicated Christians thought their gifted son wouldn't get suitable training in our school, so they sent him to local public schools. Now they wish they had that decision to make over again. Perhaps a Christian-based education would have left him with a better foundation of faith.

This young man did not lose his faith because there were not answers to the false claims of evolutionary education; he lost his faith because he was not exposed to them as he pursued his degree.

The story is too long to recount in this book, but anyone who digs into the history of education will find that educators of the religion of secularism have gravitated toward the fields of political science and law. Consequently, our once-great legal system has been turned inside out and produced lawyers who, as judges and politicians, adjudicate and legislate practices concerning values that are out of sync with the intentions of our founding fathers.

Liberal judges give such lenient sentences to violent criminals that for many our judicial system has become a joke. Such sentences have contributed to the violence on our streets, which is, in turn, leading to citizen initiatives and amendments to state constitutions that will force the police and courts to defend law-abiding citizens from criminals. William Blackstone, the great Christian jurist, whose books used to be the most studied in the field of law, has been replaced by liberal legal professors who base their thinking on the erroneous belief in the "perfectibility of man." Today's law professors largely disregard the biblical teaching that man is fallen and in need of redemption.

Liberal humanists now seem to dominate the fields of art, journalism, and communication, which are powerful and uniquely able to spread anti-Christian thought. Judge their success for yourself—just watch some of the morally defective programming in television, movies, and art displays, which are often filled with sex, infidelity, violence, and dishonesty. Where were these people educated? Probably not in private or Christian schools!

WHAT WE CAN DO

The moral degradation our culture has experienced in the last fifty years is enough evidence to prove that the secularizing of our nation's 45 million public schoolchildren and 13 million college students is extremely harmful to the future of this country and to the Christian faith of the next generation. Perhaps those late eighteenth-century humanists, atheists, free thinkers, and socialists who assumed control of public education were driven by altruistic motives. But regardless of their motives, you don't have to be extremely brilliant to see that the results have been damaging to American culture.

Those who would deny our children the right to pray to the God who created them are teaching our children that they are no more than animals, the product of evolution. In removing from our school walls the Ten Commandments, they have removed the cornerstone that has served for centuries as the foundation for harmonious society.

Christian Schools: An Alternative

Will Christians rise to the challenge to rescue our nation from the clutches of professional secularizers who masquerade as "educators"? Will we rise up and invest whatever is necessary to provide Christian school alternatives? We have the necessary buildings, most of which are idle Monday through Friday. We have the educators, and our Christian colleges could turn out many more. We have excellent curricula that educate young people both academically and morally. And we have the responsibility to raise up our children in the nurture and admonition of the Lord.

As the founders of one of the largest Christian school systems in the country (the Christian Unified School System of San Diego), we know it can be done. What it takes is a pastor who is sick of losing his young people to the world and a congregation willing to make Christian education part of its missionary ministry to families and children. Like Horace Mann, we too have a vision for this nation's schoolchildren. We want all our nation's children to have the option of being educated from kindergarten through twelfth grade in a Christian environment with a biblically based curriculum that teaches moral absolutes. That kind of education flourished for the first 250 years of our nation's history, and there's no reason it wouldn't produce moral, bright, motivated students today. "School choice" and dedicated Christian leadership can make that dream come true and help restore our nation's conscience—or at least restore the conscience of our Christian young people.

Support the Efforts to Establish a Voucher System

Christian leaders are recognizing that children who can't read or act in a morally civilized manner are victims of our secular school system, and every year we gain more advocates for the Christian school movement. We need thousands more. It is our dream that a day will come when every child who wants a Christian education will be able to get one. School choice and tuition vouchers would make that dream possible. There is nothing unconstitutional about the government giving a voucher to parents to cash at the school of their choice—religious or secular, public or private. That voucher would enable churches and religious groups all over the nation to offer a refreshing alternative to modern secular education. And it would halt the moral hemorrhaging of our nation.

Vote in the Right People

But as important as Christian schools are, we can't forget the importance of voting to save our educational system. But to maintain a godly educational foundation, it is essential that we break the present stranglehold the high priests of secularism—humanist educators—have on our educational system. Christians who realize it is time to overhaul education must get out on election day and vote into office legislators who share our moral values. We must overhaul education by approving school choice, which was advocated by the last two secretaries of education. We cannot allow the secularists in education to silence our conscience for one more day.

our
conscience
ravaged:

8

Help us to save free conscience from the paw
Of hireling wolves, whose gospel is their maw.
JOHN MILTON[1]

Milton's quote is a metaphor; he compared "hirelings," or mercenaries, to ravenous, cruel wolves whose primary instinct is to feed their own appetite. Wolves have no conscience. "Hirelings" care more for the advancement of their own goals than for the welfare of others. Nowhere are such goals more blatantly revealed than in the media, and few

179

things have done more to ravage the conscience of our nation than the entertainment industry.

OUR UNBALANCED NEWS MEDIA

At a time when America needs a balanced and truthful media, we find that the majority of our nation's radio, press, and television industry is controlled by amoral or antimoral people who use their influence to steer this country's thinking to the left. In morals, politics, education, or religion, the media seems to treat morally committed individuals and groups as the enemy. Anyone on the right is to be feared or discredited lest they become too influential. Anyone on the left is to be protected and treated with compassion. Where is the conscience of the national media?

As we write this chapter, an illustration of the media's bias is being revealed before our very eyes. Colonel Oliver North, decorated as a war hero while he was a young marine officer during the Vietnam War, is a candidate for the U.S. Senate in the state of Virginia. The media—from Ted Koppel to Tom Brokaw and all the other talking heads of television fame—has bombarded him for "lying to Congress." They neglect to tell the rest of the story.

In contrast, however, the president of the United States has been so often accused of infidelity and of lying to the public that *Reader's Digest* wrote an article entitled "Please Mr. President, Tell the Truth." David Broder, a liberal journalist, asked the same question in an article for *The Washington Post*.

While many today have found inconsistencies in what President Clinton has told the public, certain members of the left-wing media have defended him by saying, "Character is not important in a president." Yet those same media pundits demand integrity from a candidate for the U.S. Senate. In other words, character is important in a senator but not in a president. It doesn't make sense until you realize the media is in agreement with President Clinton's politics. Colonel North's conservative politics, however, they fear.

The issue is not lying; obviously the liberal members of the media don't care about lies or even adultery because, sad to say, they have grown accustomed to such behavior among government officials. The issue is philosophy. Senator Metzenbaum, a liberal politician, spoke for all liberals when he wrote in a fund-raising letter for the Democratic Party, "The greatest fear of the left can be summed up in five words—Colonel North, United States Senator!"

Liberals in the media attack any conservative who would use his influence to bring traditional values back to this country. Many of them fought President Reagan's conservative views for eight long years.

OUR MEDIA IS UNASHAMEDLY LIBERAL

All one has to do is read the daily newspapers or watch network television newscasts to understand their heavy leanings toward liberal politics. Some are more liberal than others, but most media leaders are liberal and much of their programming reflects anti-Christian sentiment.

Two sociologists, S. Robert Lichter and Stanley Rothman, under the authority of the Research Institute on International Change at Columbia University, conducted a study on *elites* in America. What these two men discovered about our supposedly free press is shocking, but it simply confirms what we have felt about the media for many years.

In their study, they conducted hour-long interviews with 240 journalists and broadcasters at the most influential media outlets: the *New York Times, The Washington Post, The Wall Street Journal, Time, Newsweek, U.S. News & World Report,* CBS, NBC, ABC, PBS, and others. They selected their interviewees at random from among reporters, columnists, department heads, bureau chiefs, editors, producers, film editors, and anchors. In addition, they interviewed business leaders at seven Fortune 500 companies, ranging from a multinational oil company to a nationwide retail chain. These interviewees were also chosen randomly to assure the accuracy of the study.

Their findings make fascinating reading. Lichter and Rothman observe:

> *The influence of the press is based not only on money or political power but on the information and ideas they transmit to other social leaders, as well as to the general public. Even those who question the media's power to persuade grant their ability to help set the agenda for discussions about social policy.*[2]

In other words, our media leaders set the agenda by selecting the subject to discuss and then inviting only those who advocate their views on programs to present their liberal views as truth. Lichter and Rothman discovered that the media elite is composed primarily of white males in the thirty- to fifty-year-old age group. One in five is a woman. Only one in twenty is not white. Nearly all have undergraduate degrees; more than half have attended graduate school. In addition to being among the best-educated individuals in America, they are also included among the most well paid.

But perhaps the most disturbing characteristic of members of the media elite is their secular outlook on life. According to Lichter and Rothman:

> *Exactly 50 percent eschew any religious affiliation. . . . Only one in five identifies himself as Protestant, and one in eight as Catholic. Very few are regular churchgoers. Only 8 percent go to church or synagogue weekly, and 86 percent seldom or never attend religious service. (p.43)*

Politically, 54 percent identify themselves as left of center; only 19 percent placed themselves on the right of the political spectrum.

> *Of those who say they voted, the proportion of leading journalists who supported the democratic presidential candidate never dropped below 80 percent. In 1972, when 62 percent of the electorate chose Nixon, 81 percent of the media elite voted for McGovern. (p. 44)*

In the Democratic landslide of 1964, Lichter and Rothman reported that the media favored Johnson over Goldwater by a margin of sixteen to one (94 percent to 6 percent)!

By an overwhelming majority, the media elite are liberals who seek to appear neutral with regard to belief in God but are typically antagonistic to anyone who believes in him. In addition, the media usually shows a strong preference for welfare capitalism. Its members do not readily admit to being socialists but are quick to advocate "a government-controlled economy" (a euphemism for socialism).

The survey demonstrated that leading journalists are most frequently strong supporters of environmental protection, affirmative action, women's rights, homosexual rights, and sexual freedom in general. In the area of personal morality, the media typically holds a distinctly amoral or pragmatic view of life. Eighty-four percent of them rejected state regulation of sexual practices; 90 percent of them agreed that a woman should have the right to an abortion; 75 percent disagreed that homosexuality is wrong; 85 percent supported the right of homosexuals to teach in schools; 54 percent did not consider adultery wrong; and only 15 percent strongly agreed that extramarital affairs are immoral.[3] This monumental survey has been supported by every similar survey taken since. Later surveys indicate that the gap between the general public and the media has widened. Why?

We believe the press has seared its conscience "as with a hot iron" (1 Tim. 4:2, NIV)—the iron of godless living.

All that many foreign countries see of America is our media programming; thus, to the outside world, America must surely seem to be a violent, immoral nation totally without a conscience. While it is true that many of our citizens have surrendered their conscience and allowed the media and the entertainment industry to think for them, we believe most Americans are not as depraved as the media portrays us.

We need voices to combat the secular voices that daily assault the American conscience, and we're grateful for the newspaper and radio producers that do allow for conservative radio programs and columnists. In the print media, the conservative *Washington Times* is published in the nation's capital, and satellite television has recently added National Empowerment Television (NET). Other local media cover various conservative issues, but these voices are few and heavily dominated by liberal news reports.

THE MORALITY GAP

Beverly and I found it fascinating to compare the Lichter and Rothman report on media perspectives to a recent study on the public's attitudes and values. This report, *The Connecticut Mutual Life Report on American Values in the 80s: The Impact of Belief,* was initiated by the Connecticut Mutual Life Insurance Company in an effort to determine the relevance of "traditional" values in our modern culture. The report "sought to identify the beliefs and attitudes of leaders, and to compare them to the public."

The researchers surveyed more than sixteen hundred people in the general public and nearly eighteen hundred leaders in the areas of business, education, government, law and justice, the military, the news media, religion, science, and voluntary associations. The researchers' discoveries were amazing. Here is what they found:

> *The impact of religious belief reaches far beyond the realm of politics, and has penetrated virtually every dimension of*

American experience. This force is rapidly becoming a more powerful factor in American life than whether someone is liberal or conservative, male or female, young or old, or a blue-collar or white-collar worker.[4]

The study revealed that although less than half of those interviewed attended church regularly, 74 percent of them considered themselves to be religious. Most shocking of all was the very clear "morality gap" that exists between the public and their leaders. As the following list shows, the leaders tend to be far more liberal in their views than the general public. Take a look at these percentages:

Percentage that believes:	Leaders	Public
Homosexuality is wrong	42%	71%
Abortion is immoral	36%	65%
Smoking marijuana is immoral	33%	57%
God loves them	54%	73%

Because our nation's leaders are among the least religious of Americans, they are out of touch with the current of faith and thought moving among the public.

Whether they are Hollywood producers, writers, or news correspondents on the evening news, most of the people who create our television shows and convey our news do not accept any absolute moral standards. Because they deny the need for a morality based upon the Word of God, they have no standard for judging what is right or wrong. They have become victims of "situation ethics," fashioning their morality as they go along. What is true today may not be true tomorrow.

WHAT FREEDOM OF THE PRESS?

Does America have freedom of the press? From government censorship, yes. But press freedom is only for the small number of liberals who control the media. Aleksandr Solzhenitsyn saw clearly the corruption of the American mass media. In his commencement address at Harvard University in 1978, Solzhenitsyn declared:

> *Enormous freedom exists for the press—but not for the readership, because newspapers mostly give stress and emphasis to those opinions which do not too sharply contradict their own, or the general trend. Without any censorship, fashionable trends of thought and ideas in the West are carefully separated from those which are not fashionable; nothing is forbidden, but what is not fashionable will hardly ever find its way into periodicals or books or be heard in the colleges.[5]*

The press, Solzhenitsyn contends, censors by ignoring those ideas or individuals not fitting the current political or social philosophy of those controlling the mass media.

As Francis Schaeffer has pointed out so well:

> *In essence, the major news organizations of the United States do not represent what can be called a free press. A free press requires the presence of organizations which compete not merely to see whether CBS, NBC, or ABC can predict the outcome of an election thirty seconds ahead of its sisters, but organizations which present distinctly and substantially different points of view.[6]*

187

It is as if members of the media are determined to "protect" the public, giving them only the information the media thinks they want to hear. If the public insists on hearing the truth about the situation on the field, the self-proclaimed protectors will tell it, grudgingly, but will clothe the truth in their own amoral, liberal style.

SELECTIVE REPORTING CONSISTENTLY FAVORS LIBERALS

During my junior year at Dartmouth College, there was a small student takeover of the administration building to protest the war in Vietnam. In the middle of the night, a friend woke me to say that the National Guard was evacuating the administration building. The landscape was empty except for a few observers like myself, a handful of National Guardsmen, the thirty students who had occupied the building, and the television news crews. However, the next day on television the operation looked like a major military maneuver. Frightened alumni and parents from all over the country started to call the college. The television news team made such tight shots of the scene in the midst of the small crowd that the event looked larger and more important than it actually was. I realized then the meaning of the axiom that a protest really occurs only if the television cameras are there.[7]

After watching the media carefully for many years, we are convinced that liberals use "the power of the press," whether television, radio, print press, or wire service, to promote other liberals and liberal causes. The first time we became aware of this was years ago when we noticed the media always spoke well of former Republican Senator Jacob Javits of New York.

188

By that time we had noticed that the press was responsible in many states for the election of liberal Democratic governors, senators, and congressmen. *The New York Times* particularly favored liberal Democrats, whether endorsing the mayor of New York City or the governor of the state.

After all, we had read in history that the *Times* "made" the career of Franklin D. Roosevelt back in the late 1920s, helping him get elected as governor of New York, the largest state in the union. After serving as governor, he was then qualified, with the *Times*'s help, to run for and win the presidency of the United States. Naturally, he repaid his patrons by changing our country forever from a basically conservative government to a very liberal one. Not only did he bring in more liberal socialist programs than any president before him, but in his twelve years in the White House he appointed more U.S. Supreme Court justices than any president since George Washington, who appointed them all. As we could expect, all of FDR's appointees were liberal. And one, Felix Frankfurter, was the first ACLU member appointed to the Court. FDR's appointees not only found "constitutional" much liberal legislation that, in fact, conflicted with "original intent," but they also changed the role of the Court. Now, instead of interpreting the Constitution, the Supreme Court misuses it by making rulings that amount to law, sometimes with strong socialistic tendencies.

In the case of Senator Javits, why would *The New York Times* be so friendly toward a Republican? The answer lies in his voting record in the Senate. He voted with liberal Democrats more often than he did his own Republican Party. The media's ideal for America's two-party system would have both candidates be liberal.

Contrast the *Times's* conduct with the equally liberal *Atlanta Constitution,* the *Constitution* that was notorious for fighting former Democratic congressman Larry MacDonald from Georgia. Dr. MacDonald had been a highly respected medical doctor before running for Congress, and every time he ran he was opposed by the *Atlanta Constitution,* even as an incumbent. While that newspaper usually endorses Democrats, they rejected MacDonald because he had a 100 percent conservative voting record. Few Republicans were his equal as a conservative. Some conservatives wonder if the unarmed civilian Korean jetliner wasn't blown out of the sky because Dr. MacDonald was on board.

Consider now the 1992 presidential campaign. President Clinton's reputation was attacked for an alleged affair with Gennifer Flowers, other allegations of sexual misconduct, and the Whitewater scandal. The media's first response was to try to manufacture a moral scandal against George Bush, but the rumors that flew around concerning President Bush proved an embarrassment even to the media. President Clinton's problems, though, wouldn't go away, but the media largely ignored the Gennifer Flowers allegations and other allegations of adultery. When the rumors refused to go away and Flowers produced a taped telephone conversation to prove her story, some in the media countered by saying that "character is not important" in a candidate, flaws they would probably not have excused in a conservative candidate if they could have been substantiated.

The Whitewater allegations may have caused the defeat

of President Clinton in the primaries had the media taken the allegations seriously. Instead of trying to get to the real truth, the media spent more time attacking the sons of George Bush for financial dealings (attacks that were mysteriously dropped after the election) than they did investigating the allegations against their candidate, Bill Clinton. L. Brent Bozell III, chairman of the Media Research Center, exposed the media's silence during the campaign because they remained silent despite the available evidence about Whitewater:

> *Now that Whitewater is on the front burner, the media would like us to think they wanted to play all along. But let's remember where the media placed themselves on this story two years ago. On March 8, 1992,* The New York Times *broke the first story about Whitewater.* The Washington Post *followed a week later with a story on the Rose Law Firm's state business. A feeding frenzy in the works? Not exactly. Over the next three weeks, the four networks filed only five full stories. In its March 23 edition,* Newsweek *reported one sentence.* Time *did nothing, and* U.S. News & World Report, *which considered it of import to publish a big report on the dealings of presidential son, George W. Bush, the week before, reported nothing on Whitewater.*[8]

Newsweek media critic Jonathan Alter—who came to the Clintons' defense when Jerry Brown, the most liberal candidate running in the Democratic primary, brought it up— said, "Hillary Clinton takes no share of state fees, but if she did, it is peanuts . . . compared to . . . Bush's sons who make

Hillary Clinton's activity look like one of those tea-and-cookies parties she disparages."⁹

Now, of course, Bush's sons have been vindicated, and at this writing both the Senate and the House of Representatives are considering holding public hearings on the serious manipulations of the Clintons. Hillary's "peanuts" turned out to be a two-thousand-dollar-a-month retainer for two years from the bank owned by her Whitewater partner.

Based on more than thirty-five years of observing the "fruits" of the media, we have no doubt they will not hesitate to use their powerful positions to help other liberals get elected to public offices from school board members to the presidency. That is why our government is far more liberal than the American people.

THE ROLE OF THE MEDIA IN THE ELECTION OF THE PRESIDENT
Politics and show business are inextricably linked.[10]

As a mother bird feeds her hungry young, so television feeds its naive viewers. In an unprecedented fashion, the 1992 presidential elections were waged in the living rooms of our nation via television. In the Bush-Clinton-Perot fight for the presidency, the winner was he who mastered the media most consistently. The winner was Bill Clinton, who gained 43 percent of the vote.

We have become a nation whose convictions are formed not in the heart or the mind but in the gut. If we *feel* that something is right or desirable, we pursue it. On the other hand, if we don't *feel* inclined toward it, we quickly dismiss it.

It's as easy and quick as the touch of a finger on a remote-control button.

But should our deep-seated loyalties and allegiances be formed in the living room in front of the television screen? And is it wise to trust our fleeting impressions in making decisions of profound importance? We never consider these questions. We are the products of a fast-food, fast-impression, fast-reaction, fast-feeling society. But we who vote in haste have four years of leisure in which to repent.

Did President Clinton win the election because he was the best candidate? Was it because he had the character Americans desire in their chief? Was it because of a sterling reputation for integrity, loyalty, and courage? Was it because he held to the values most Americans cherish? For many Americans— including some who voted for him—each of these questions would perhaps receive a different answer now, after the election.

President Clinton was elected because he mastered the media. He had friends in high places in the television world. Harry Thomason, a friend of Bill Clinton's for twenty years, and his wife and partner, Linda Bloodworth-Thomason, producer of sitcoms such as *Designing Women, Evening Shade,* and *Hearts Afire,* were invaluable sources of support to the candidate throughout his rocky campaign. During the New Hampshire primaries, when Clinton the candidate was suffering the aftermath of allegations of sexual impropriety, the Thomasons stuck by him. In fact, the Thomason connection afforded the Clintons an opportunity for a Barbara Walters interview. As we could expect, Barbara Walters lobbed softball questions to the Clintons, opening doors for him to explain away his affairs. That was a significant event in the campaign and was partly responsible for Clinton's improved ratings among American television viewers.

In an interview with *TV Guide,* President Clinton acknowledged the importance of the television in his winning the election. "When people look back at this year and ask, 'What really happened?' I think two-way communication on television between the candidate and the people will be the story."[11]

TV Guide itself acknowledges the role the media played in the election. These words open an article entitled "Clinton on Television":

> *In 1992, the critical skills of presidential politics became indistinguishable from television's key skills—why to avoid Dan Rather, when to chat with Larry King, how to hold a cordless mike, where to take viewers' call-in questions. Bill Clinton, the first of his baby-boom television generation to run for the White House, mastered them all as he took the top prize on November 3. In the process, politics and television were transformed forever.[12]*

It would be one thing if the contest involved athletes and actors and the victor gained a prize or public recognition. But when it comes to the presidency of our nation, woe to us if television performance determines the outcome. Presidential media advisers were not political "handlers" as before but Hollywood sitcom producers. Is America just a real-life sitcom? We hope not! Yet we fear that many of our countrymen are mesmerized by the media and are becoming intellectually and morally anemic through excessive television ingestion.

What Clinton advisers appreciated about television was the opportunity to finesse their way out of the problems of reality. It enabled him to deal with difficult problems by refocusing the issues, and he did it with ease and fluidity on television. Such was not the case with then-President Bush, whose loss *TV Guide* attributes to his slowness in appreciating television's uses. "Bush watched his opponent's ratings rise as he sat out the race in the Rose Garden,"[13] the magazine scornfully observed.

DARK CLOUDS DESCEND OVER THE CLINTON ADMINISTRATION

In 1983 the two of us had a private interview with Ted Turner in his Atlanta office. Even then his CNN television network was making an impact on the communications industry. During the interview he said, "Television is the most powerful force in America!"

We asked, "What about government? It is certainly powerful."

Turner didn't hesitate to emphatically reply: "Television is *more* powerful than the government. It *elects* the government!"

Pat Buchanan, conservative journalist and spokesman, has been a member of the media all of his adult life. He was a speechwriter for Presidents Nixon and Reagan and is a syndicated columnist. In a *Washington Times* piece entitled "Big Media Go Easy on Clinton," he decries the double standard of hard-line liberals in media. They tore apart Clarence Thomas, whose sole accuser had confusing and unsubstantiated testimony. Due to media manipulation, Justice Thomas's appointment was nearly shipwrecked. Why? Because Clarence Thomas is a conservative.

On the other hand, any logical person must ask why Bill Clinton is being protected in the face of so many accusations by credible individuals who are willing to be identified and whose testimonies substantiate each other. Why has their testimony been stonewalled by the press? Because Bill Clinton is their mascot. In the face of their disastrously unprofessional treatment of the many accusations against a liberal president, Patrick Buchanan writes:

> *If the media wish to understand the minimum high regard in which they are held by their countrymen, they might reflect upon the double standard by which they judge public men.*
>
> *Does anyone believe, for example, the Big Media would have sloughed it off as unworthy of follow-up if Maine state troopers claimed President Bush had called them and bartered jobs for silence?*
>
> *What's going on here? Simple. The Big Media have a vested interest in the Clinton presidency, having tossed aside any pretense of neutrality to get him elected. Since they arrived, Bill and Hillary Rodham Clinton have been cut slack never cut for Ronald and Nancy Reagan.*
>
> *Mickey Kaus, of* The New Republic, *admits it: "Clinton is the best president we've had in a long time. That is the unspoken reason the sex charges haven't received as much play as you might expect."*
>
> *Bill's their boy, and Hillary's their gal. That's why we don't see any of the old tallyho spirit of the chase that Ben Bradlee so beautifully exemplified when, as Iran-contra crashed on*

Reagan's head, he exulted, "We haven't had this much fun since Watergate!"

Not much fun this time, is it, fellas? [14]

In politics it is no longer "let the best man win." Today the winner is the one who comes across television best, the one the liberal "talking heads" and talk-show hosts like most. The "spin" of the media can sway 10 percent or more of the voters, and barring a miracle, we are in for a succession of very liberal leaders.

FROM POLITICS TO ENTERTAINMENT, THE MEDIA ELITE DOMINATE

It is obvious to anyone who examines the facts that the most powerful voice of conscience today is the entertainment industry, based primarily in Hollywood and New York. The "artists-as-conscience" trend started later than the other agencies of humanism, but today these unelected hedonistic "artists" virtually control 90 percent of the most powerful and influential vehicle to the human mind ever invented—film.

Film, whether a movie on television, at the theater, or on video, bombards both the eyes and the ears as it assaults the minds, emotions, and morals of our 250 million citizens, or at least those who watch them. Unfortunately, far too many Christians have lowered their standards in regard to their selection of movies or television shows, and this influential industry has affected the values and mores of many Christians.

Having been in church work all our life, we find it painful

197

to admit that the men and women in the entertainment industry have more influence on the conscience of our nation than do preachers, parents, teachers, or anyone else. In fact, it is a very small group of individuals who hold our nation's morals hostage. Less than a few thousand movie studio owners, producers, television station and network owners, actors, and others control this morally uncontrolled industry whose greatest victims are our nation's children. There is no more powerful tool in the battle for our culture than the entertainment industry, most of whose members have adopted the values of secularism.

Based on their movies and television productions, the morals of the entertainment industry have mirrored the amoral standards of secularism and have gone rapidly downhill. Today films not only glorify the immoral, but promote the antimoral.

The problem is compounded when the media turns to these "role models" for advice on the burning issues of the day and gives them a national audience to communicate their antimoral ideas.

Elizabeth Taylor, the eight-times-married movie star of yesteryear, often pops up on national shows to offer her ideas on subjects ranging from AIDS to virtue. Donald Trump, the divorced New York playboy and casino owner, was recently featured with his new wife, a woman he lived with who broke up his first marriage, on the front cover of *Vanity Fair* to offer his views on "family values." Even before reading the article, you know he doesn't understand the "family values" that you and I revere, traditional moral values that helped make this the greatest country on earth.

ENTERTAINMENT INDUSTRY AS THE NATION'S CONSCIENCE

In much of the world . . . where dictators are dumped and walls crash down, the picture seems brighter, but in my local video store, I see teenagers stockpiling at least ten hours of horror, porn, and pain for the weekend. . . . Alone in a darkened space our moral sensibilities are no match for the Tinseltown hype and the whiz-bang reviews. . . . As surely as toxic residue kills the fish and the fowl, so the sloth of our mean-spirited film-makers and writers kills our spirit. It is renewal that is needed now.—Richard Neville[15]

Ever since Clark Gable uttered the "d" word for the first time on screen in *Gone with the Wind*, profanity has gradually eroded decent speech so that today it is the rule rather than the exception. Most films out of Hollywood today use profanity as though everyone talks that way. Though the profanity usually adds nothing to the story line, it has come to be expected in movies and is now common on late-night television and increasingly tolerated in prime time.

What else are our children watching on television? Morality in Media tells us:

By the time the average child graduates from elementary school, she or he will have witnessed at least 8,000 murders and more than 100,000 other assorted acts of violence on television. Depending on the amount of television viewed, some youngsters could see more than 200,000 violent acts before they hit the schools and streets of our nation as teenagers.[16]

Ted Baehr, a Christian who has been active in television production since 1972, says that violence on television "mainstreams" an audience in three different ways: Some viewers are not overtly affected at all, some become anxious and worried about the world, and some are attracted by the violence, sometimes to the degree that they emulate it in the real world.[17]

But the first group, those who are not overtly affected, cannot escape television's influence. Baehr writes:

> *Recent research has confirmed Marshall McLuhan's prediction that the "media explosion" would cause most people to experience a "perceptual numbing," "a stubborn insensitivity to all but the most extreme experiences in life." Dr. Robert Coles, a child psychiatrist at Harvard University, has found that children are particularly susceptible to perceptual numbing, and those children who watch a great deal of television turn off their minds to what they are watching.*[18]

Most of us are numbed by violence on television, another group of us is made paranoid, and another group is actually enthralled by the vile practices on the screen! At a time when the incidences of murder, rape, and even child molestation are increasing, the keepers of the entertainment industry in Hollywood are producing films that many claim educate viewers about how to perform such vile acts. Producers deny that they are responsible for the acts of violence they inspire, but evidence shows that in real life many people do imitate what they see. Throughout America many "copycat" crimes have left victims dead or maimed for life.

While we are discussing powerful influences, we cannot ignore the rock music industry. The obscene, immoral, and blasphemous lyrics, along with the suggestive and blatant gestures of rock stars, influence many young people to follow those immoral lifestyles. Rock musicians are consistent in their disdain and irreverent treatment of Jesus Christ. For instance, in *The Advocate* newspaper, Madonna said: "I think they probably got it on, Jesus and Mary Magdalene."[19]

The music of the forties and fifties was about love, companionship, and the heartbreak of love. It certainly was not Christian music, but the songs did not encourage immoral acts or blaspheme Jesus Christ. Today's rock stars have become idols and role models for many of our youth. Teens listen to hours of blasphemous words from heavy metal rock stars—the more blasphemous the lyrics, the larger are the crosses the stars hang around their neck. In May of 1985 Madonna told *Spin* magazine: "Crucifixes are sexy because there's a naked man on them."

The movie industry wasn't always profane either. In 1933 Cardinal Dougherty of Philadelphia saw a lurid billboard advertising a Warner Brothers picture, and so he asked his church to boycott Warner Brothers. Filmmakers did not want to lose a large segment of a righteous, religious, moviegoing public, so they banded together and asked churchmen to form the Legion of Decency to benefit moviegoers and filmmakers alike. The Legion and Protestant Film Office influenced the motion picture industry for thirty-five years through the Motion Picture Code.

During that time religion-oriented films saved the studios from financial ruin. In 1959 *Ben Hur* saved MGM from bankruptcy, just as *The Ten Commandments* had saved Paramount from a similar fate in 1956. *A Man Called Peter,* a movie based on the life of Senate Chaplain Peter Marshall, was another tremendous success.[20]

But in 1966 each member of the Legion withdrew from the organization for various reasons, and the burden of discretion was shifted from movie studios to audiences. In 1968 the Motion Picture Association of America established a rating system that allows for virtually anything today.[21]

Most of the families that originated the great Hollywood film studios are no longer living, and the industry has been bought by industrial conglomerates like General Electric (NBC), foreigners, and Ted Turner—whose current wife, Jane Fonda, is anything but an advocate of traditional, biblically based values.

The content of entertainment has steadily declined, while special effects and techniques have made remarkably rapid advances, enabling producers to make their morally hostile messages even more dangerous and appealing to young viewers. Today, many of our youth adopt their moral standards from movies and music. MTV has made it possible to merge both television and rock music with the attendant evils of both. No wonder promiscuity and profanity have reached frightening proportions!

Hollywood Hates Christianity

The greatest sin of Hollywood is blasphemy. The names of God and his Son, Jesus Christ, are invoked frequently in one form of profanity or another. You will remember that one of the Ten Commandments warns that "the Lord will not leave him unpunished who takes His name in vain" (Exod. 20:7). We have often wondered if some of the stark Hollywood tragedies have had anything to do with the industry's haphazard blasphemy.

Hollywood's hatred of God is also apparent in other forms. The elite attack religious people and clergy with a vengeance. Michael Medved, a devout Jew, is a film critic who has refused to sacrifice his moral values and deeply held religious beliefs for professional gain. In his book *Hollywood v. America,* he illustrates how today's movies attack Christian doctrines. The following review of the film *The Rapture* (1991) appeared in Michael Medved's book:

> *Mimi Rogers plays a buxom swinger, addicted to group sex with strangers, who sacrifices these satisfactions when she makes a sudden commitment to Christ. At first, her religious transformation appears to have positive consequences, but before the end of the film her "faith" causes her to take her six-year-old daughter out to the desert where they wait for days in the burning sun for the Rapture that is supposed to precede Christ's second coming. When nothing happens, the heroine takes a revolver, holds it to her daughter's head, and, while mumbling invocations of the Almighty, blows the child's brains out.*
>
> *Throughout the film, Christian believers are portrayed as twitching zombies, with an obvious edge of madness behind their fervent beliefs. The only church you ever see in the film is a cultish congregation of about a dozen leisure-suited losers who worship an eleven-year-old African-American "prophet" who barks out weird metaphysical commands like a pint-*

sized Jim Jones. Naturally, those who belittle religious think-ing deliver all the best lines. For instance, when the main character first displays her interest in Christianity, her boy-friend tells her, "It's like a drug. You feel pain. So instead of doing heroin, you do God." At the end of the film, after murdering her daughter, this tormented woman at last dis-covers the "courage" to blame God (who else?) for her own mad act. "You're supposed to love God no matter what," she declares. "But I don't love him anymore. He has too many rules."

In an interview after the film's release, writer-director Michael Tolkin explained that he had altered the ending of the picture to make the antireligious message even more unequivocal. In the original version of the picture, the heroine "realized she made a mistake and she wants to go to heaven." Film maker Tolkin believes that final version features a character who is "stronger" because "she's rejecting God for creating a universe that put her to the test in the first place."

In another interview, Jim Svejda of CBS Radio asked Tolkin about charges that his film unfairly attacked religious believers. "It's not anti-religion," he answered. "It's anti-God." [22]

One wonders how one can be *for* religion, but *against* God.

THE BLASPHEMOUS MOVIE
THE LAST TEMPTATION OF CHRIST

Christians are particularly incensed when Hollywood blas-phemes their Lord, and a recent blatant attempt to blaspheme Christ was Martin Scorsese's controversial box office bomb

The Last Temptation of Christ. We could not bring ourselves to view it; reading the reviews was bad enough. But because twenty-five thousand Christians demonstrated at Universal Studios in protest, Michael Medved did review it. You'll understand the depths to which Hollywood plummeted by reading his review:

> *As the controversy intensified in the days immediately prior to the film's release, I tried to focus on my job as a movie critic and to stay away from the increasingly hysterical theological and constitutional debates. I wanted to see* The Last Temptation of Christ *with an open mind and to assess its artistic excellence (or inadequacy) as a motion picture, rather than surveying its importance as a battleground in the ongoing culture war. As a practicing Jew, I could sympathize with the sense of violation and outrage that many of my Christian friends felt as soon as they heard about the film, but I never shared their visceral reaction; nor did I experience the similarly passionate (and similarly instinctive) impulse of some industry insiders who rushed to the defense of the film the moment it was attacked by the religious right.*
>
> *With these intense emotions very much in the air, I gathered with a dozen other critics to see the picture at a weekday afternoon screening two weeks before its release. . . .*
>
> *Unfortunately, as* The Last Temptation of Christ *unreeled before our astonished eyes, it became clear almost immediately that he might have retitled this new film* Raging Messiah. *Within its first five minutes the picture offers a sequence in which Jesus (Willem Dafoe) inexplicably assists the Romans in crucifying some innocent Jewish victim. . . .*

205

Such graphic and shocking gore recurs at regular intervals, providing the only relief to long, arid stretches of appalling boredom, laughable dialogue, and unbearably bad acting. Even those who publicly praised the film confessed that its two-hour-and-forty-four minute running time amounted to something of an ordeal for the audience; I found the entire experience as uplifting and rewarding as two hours and forty-four minutes in the dentist's chair. . . . Some of my generally restrained colleagues, who attended the same critics' screening I did, began snickering, hooting, and laughing aloud midway through the picture's all-but-insufferable length.

When we finally staggered out into the light of day, blinking our eyes and shaking our heads in disbelief, a television camera crew from a national entertainment show approached a few of the recognizable reviewers in the crowd and asked for our instantaneous responses. I told them, "It is the height of irony that all this controversy should be generated by a film that turns out to be so breathtakingly bad, so unbearably boring. In my opinion, the controversy about this picture is a lot more interesting than the film itself." . . . I stand by the comment today, not only as an expression of my own opinion, but as an accurate summary of the general reaction of those who sat beside me in that screening room and watched the film for the first time that afternoon.

I was therefore amazed and appalled in the days that followed at the generally respectful—even reverential—tone that so many of my colleagues adopted in their reviews. In particular, I found it impossible to understand the one critic who had snorted the loudest and clucked the most derisively at the afternoon screening we both attended, but whose ultimate report to the public featured glowing praise and only the most minor reservations.

When I called him to ask about the contrast between his privately expressed contempt and his on-the-record admiration, he proved surprisingly candid in explaining his inconsistency. "Look, I know the picture's a dog," he said. "We both know that, and probably Scorsese knows it, too. But with all the Christian crazies shooting at him from every direction, I'm not going to knock him in public. If I slammed the picture too hard, then people would associate me with Falwell—and there's no way I'm ready for that."

I believe that his confidential comments offer the best explanation for the utterly undeserved critical hosannas that the picture provoked. . . .

In a sense, the response to the film (including Scorsese's surprise nomination for an Academy Award as Best Director, and official endorsements by the Writers Guild, the Directors Guild, and the Motion Picture Association of America) represented the movie industry's "circle the wagons" mentality at its most hysterical and paranoid. Veteran star Mickey Rooney, one of the few established Hollywood figures to speak up against Scorsese's acclaimed "masterpiece," concluded: "The Last Temptation of Christ *provides a good example of the film establishment rallying around a bad film to protect its own selfish interest. . . . That film, no matter what its defenders say, was a slap in the face to Christians everywhere, but Hollywood cradled the picture as if it were* Citizen Kane." *When religious figures across the country attacked the picture, the members of the Hollywood community felt called upon to close ranks and to do rhetorical battle with any who dared criticize the industry and its values.*

That's why so many of the film's supporters not only praised it as a work of art, but defended it as an act of faith. . . . The public wisely ignored such glowing notices and the film quickly developed the deadly word-of-mouth it so richly deserved. . . . Though precise figures will never be made public, best estimates indicate that Universal's overall loss on the project could hardly have been less than $10 million—an appalling result for a project that had received the most lavish prerelease in modern motion picture history.[23]

The movie industry would *never* purposely offend homosexuals, native Americans, environmentalists, animal rights activists, or women's groups, but they don't think twice about something that might offend Christians. In fact, the Hollywood elite seem to get great enjoyment out of trampling our values in the mud. We may never know how many lives have rotted in the trash heap of moral debauchery because of the antimoral, anti-Christian diatribes they call "art."

Michael Medved again recognized Hollywood's inconsistency when he reviewed another attack on Christianity, the movie *Cape Fear:*

What surprised me most about the wildly enthusiastic critical response to the film at the time of its release was that so few of my colleagues took note of this connection, or joined me in pointing out the movie's defamatory treatment of committed Christians. Imagine that the picture had portrayed the vengeful psychotic as a member of some other group known for its abiding faith and passionate commitment—say the ACLU, or Greenpeace, or the National Abortion Rights Action League, or the AIDS Coalition to Unleash Power, or the American Indian Movement. Wouldn't his identification with one of these causes or lifestyles seem an absolutely unnecessary affront to all others who shared such values? Why, then, should industry insiders so cheerfully accept the decision to make the evil maniac an evangelical Christian?

Just a few months before Universal released Cape Fear, *the entertainment press and the studio establishment gave respectful treatment to representatives of GLAAD (The Gay and Lesbian Alliance Against Discrimination) who protested the movie* The Silence of the Lambs. *They complained that in portraying a brutal serial killer (Ted Levine) with effeminate mannerisms (and a poodle named Precious), the movie perpetuated hateful stereotypes and slandered all gay people. Why is it offensive to portray a creep and a murderer as a homosexual, but totally acceptable to present him as a religious Christian? The contrast between the serious discussion of the potentially offensive content in* The Silence of the Lambs *and the total silence concerning the possibility of antireligious bigotry in* Cape Fear, *or* Misery, *or so many other films highlights the irrational double standard that afflicts nearly all industry insiders.*[24]

MOVIES FUEL TELEVISION

Whether or not you attend movies at the theater, you must be concerned about them because sooner or later they will find their way to television and your living room. What

Hollywood sanctions today, the country will probably sanction tomorrow.

Morality in Media reports that the average American household watches seven hours and forty-one minutes of television per day. Adults watch an average of four hours and forty-nine minutes, teens watch an average of three hours and six minutes, and children watch an average of three hours and thirty minutes of television per day. In fact, up to 12 percent of television viewers consider themselves addicted to television! This is particularly disturbing in light of the programming currently available on television.

THE NOT-SO-SUBTLE TEACHING TECHNIQUES OF TELEVISION

There is no greater illustration of how Hollywood has replaced the church as the conscience of the nation than in the field of moral values. As everyone knows, the Bible and the church have always stood for morality in life, monogamy and commitment in marriage, and a heterosexual lifestyle. Men marry women and women marry men. But Hollywood more and more reflects other values. Even in the "golden age of Hollywood," its stars were often personally immoral, though studio execs tried to keep the stars' adultery and homosexuality hidden from the public and limited immorality's expression on the screen.

Gradually, though, those barriers were broken down, and the immorality of Hollywood evolved into standard movie plots. Today anything goes. There is a total disregard for moral values and absolutes. In fact, in the Hollywood world of fantasy, moral behavior is separated from character. We are urged to root for the "good guy" or the heroine even though he or she is having an affair or sleeping with someone on the first date. Hollywood refuses to acknowledge that character produces moral behavior and that a lack of character is at the root of sin.

A case in point is an old detective series that is now coming back on cable: "Spencer for Hire." Spencer was a good guy, Mister Clean. In the days of cowboy flicks he would have worn a white hat. He was smarter than the police and was impeccably honest. And, of course, as a detective, Spencer always "got his man."

Good old Spencer just has one problem. He is immoral and sleeps with his girlfriend on weekends. And therein lies the subtlety. The entertainment industry is instructing a watching public that a person's sexual behavior is separate from his character. People who violate God's commands in one area will do the same in others.

Another popular detective show in the 1980s featured a very capable actor who always confounded the police and solved the case brilliantly. He was tough, good-looking, honest, and lived an impeccable life—except for his sexual behavior. With that regard, he had the morals of an alley cat, to put it nicely. Again, we're seeing Hollywood's equation of success with promiscuity and a lack of marital commitment. Programs such as that do more than just kill time; they send the subliminal message that we ought to "go and do likewise."

One night we were watching a public interest program and saw an interview with the producer of the show we just mentioned. Suddenly we understood why our alley-cat detective was constantly on the prowl! This producer really hated women! He had never had a good relationship with a woman in his life—from the mother who rejected him to any of his five wives—and was living in a world of sexual fantasy. Much of television today is, like that show, the work of producers who find satisfaction in using television to broadcast their sexually filthy fantasies into the homes of 250 million Americans. The damage inflicted in living color on the minds of unsuspecting viewers—particularly youth—is nothing short of devastating. Can anyone doubt that such visualized fancies are having an effect today?

THE HYPOCRISY OF THE MEDIA

Nowhere is the hypocrisy of liberalism—or, if you prefer, secularism—more apparent than in the unpatriotic preference for marxism and left-wing dictatorships depicted in movies and films for television. Directors can find much wrong with America, like Oliver Stone spewing forth his hatred and disillusionment with America and the Vietnam War. And they find much wrong with institutions that children should be taught to respect.

It is, for example, hard for Hollywood to portray a good cop in detective or police shows without also showing the cop with questionable values. Hollywood heavies are almost as hard on the police as they are on religious leaders. At a time when being a police officer is the most dangerous profession in the country, they are not exalting these heroic and valiant people who keep the peace in society. Instead, they exalt the errors.

It is a moral outrage that these filmmakers are so reticent to make films that do not flatter the liberal, brutal regimes of

212

the world. When it comes to taking sides, Hollywood personalities usually take up the cause of the enemies of America. During the Vietnam War, starlet Jane Fonda went to Hanoi and spoke out against her country and the American prisoners there, earning her the nickname "Hanoi Jane." Although she later offered a mild apology for what she did, she is still not popular among the former prisoners whose torture was increased as a result of her visit.

And now that the Soviet system has collapsed, revealing the criminality and human destruction that went on behind the Iron Curtain, Hollywood is practically silent. I cannot believe that hundreds of gripping movies could not have been made featuring the intrigue of the KGB and Soviet spies as they sought to advance communism. Hollywood seems to care most about the profits they make in peddling sex and violence.

Many people would listen to the voice of conscience if they knew what channel it was on.[25]

WHAT WE CAN DO

1. Turn it off! Television sets that are not turned on can't harm anyone. We must take our own share of the responsibility for programming that comes into our homes. If we allow children to watch unbridled, then they will gravitate to the wrong kind of programming. Many Christian homes are finding it easier to get rid of the family television set altogether. But because some programming is often good and wholesome, less drastic measures seem more reasonable for most homes. The best way to help children with television viewing is to set

213

a good example. If children find their parents up late watching pornographic videos or cable programs, the parents are surrendering their moral authority to tell their children what they should and shouldn't watch. And when producers offend your moral values, make their programming off-limits to your whole family.

2. Make them pay! We can stop supporting advertisers of unwholesome programming by boycotting products and letting the manufacturers know you are doing so. One filthy TV show on ABC has been targeted by Don Wildmon and his American Family Association, and the TV show can't find advertisers. So far, it has cost the network over $17 million.

3. Teach your children how to filter the media: Parents could make it a point to watch certain programming and movies together and after the viewing discuss the good and bad about what they have seen and heard. Central to the discussion should be a question and answer session, such as, What do you think the people who wrote that program believe about God? about absolute truth? How did the philosophies agree or disagree with what you know about God and the Bible? And finally, Is this the kind of thing we, as Christians, ought to be using to fill our mind?

In conclusion, we should not blame the government, secular humanism, the media, or its writers and directors for immoral teaching unless we are ready to do our part to stop the flow or to find better alternatives for ourselves and our children. Hopefully, a consortium of Christian entrepreneurs will catch the vision for buying one of the TV networks and for using twenty-first-century technology to establish a conservative newspaper for the major cities of the country. Until

Christians, religious citizens, and others interested in traditional values create a TV and newspaper network for family-oriented citizens (which comprise the majority of our population), we will continue to be led astray by the secularist minority who control our nation's major means of communication.

our
conscience
renewed:

9

*Conscience tells us that we ought to do right, but it does not tell
us what right is; that we are taught by God's Word.*
                                        HENRY CLAY TRUMBULL[1]

America's problems did not spring upon us without warning. It took the influence of liberals more than 150 years
to destroy the foundations laid for this country by our predominantly Christian forefathers. Obviously it will take a
long time to return it to the moral base upon which it was
established. But our nation's moral conscience, which is so

desperately needed today, will never be renewed by liberals. Not only have their ideas perpetrated the destruction of our nation's moral base and conscience, but also liberals today don't seem to recognize their role in the social chaos of our current society.

Liberals are concerned about the results of sin: escalating out-of-wedlock births, sexually transmitted diseases, AIDS, drug-crazed millions, violence, murder, school dropouts, and academic decline. But they don't seem to make the connection that it was some of their liberal policies that are at fault. They spend their time fighting the "religious right," "the new right," Concerned Women for America, the Christian Coalition, "Protestant fundamentalists," conservatives of every stripe, and anyone of influence who opposes liberalism or secularism. They prefer to promote "the Gay Agenda," pornography, socialized medicine, government-planned everything (socialism by another name), the ACLU, freedom for liberals to dominate the educational system from kindergarten to the doctoral level, and the campaign to further secularize our country.

Since liberals have no clue what is causing our river of life to be polluted, we cannot count on them to cure the problem. A national cure can only come as sufficient numbers of concerned citizens begin to understand how harmful man-centered programs have been and that their own negligence has opened the door for elements responsible for the destruction of the morals and conscience of our nation. With God's grace, if 20 percent of Christians who are now seemingly passive would become involved by becoming informed, registering to vote, voting, and praying, some of the trends toward further immorality could be stopped.

Christians need to understand, however, that we are the only group in this country large enough to do that. True, many politically conservative citizens will help, and the current administration's policies are very likely to activate a new conservative movement as did the liberal Kennedy and Johnson administrations in the 1960s.

Liberals fear the religious right because they know their enormous numbers pose a threat to the liberals' continued influence on our society. They know that Gallup polls indicate that 38 percent (as many as 69 million) Americans are evangelicals. They also know that evangelicals are more evangelistic than liberal Protestants, so our numbers grow each year. Liberals also recognize what they consider a dangerous phenomenon: When some from their midst become Christians and begin to attend Bible-teaching churches, they most often begin to vote for the conservative platform and for conservative candidates.

For this reason, liberals try to discredit and destroy Christian leaders at every turn. Their savage attack on attorney Mike Farris in his run for lieutenant governor of Virginia in 1993 was a classic example: By distorting Farris's views on prayer, education, and religious freedom, they managed to portray him as a wide-eyed radical member of the religious right. Their plan succeeded, and they were able to block his election. Pat Robertson received the same treatment in his bid for the White House in 1988. Christians can expect such treatment all over the country, but that should not deter those who feel called of God to run for office. Some of them do win!

Recently Tim sat next to Congressman Tim Hutchinson on an airplane to Washington, D.C. The congressman recognized him and introduced himself, saying, "In 1984 I read your book, *The Battle for the Mind,* and it convinced me that as a Christian, I should run for public office." Just 150 more like him in the House and 20 more in the Senate would not only halt the current liberal stranglehold on our government but would also help restore some degree of moral conscience to our nation's public policy.

WHY WE MUST HAVE HOPE

On May 10, 1987, Ted Koppel, anchor of the news program *Nightline,* did something that surprised many of us: He spoke out against the erosion of morals in this country. During his graduation day address at Duke University, he confronted the graduates with the concept of moral absolutes—one with which many were no doubt unfamiliar, having been raised on moral relativism. "What Moses brought down from Mount Sinai were not the Ten Suggestions. They are commandments," Koppel asserted.

As a result of secular humanist education, our nation has so indulged itself that we are on the verge of anarchy. Until the 1960s, we expected some degree of morality to be the norm. Having known the pre–1960s America, Koppel, apparently disillusioned by the depraved condition of many of his countrymen, was firmly persuaded that we need to take seriously the ten laws that had formed the basis for our legal system. He realized that the universal standard for civility was based on the Ten Commandments recorded by Moses. No other set of laws before or since can compare with this succinct collection of God-inspired laws. Concurring with this thought, Koppel also noted that "the sheer brilliance of the Ten Commandments is that they codify in a handful of words acceptable human behavior, not just for then or now, but for all time."

There has never been a better standard for human behavior than the Ten Commandments, but the majority of the liberal elite reject this standard because it comes from the Bible. It is illegal to so much as post the Ten Commandments on the walls of some of our public schools. As the Ten Commandments were expelled from our schools, sane and safe behavior was replaced by guns, violence, promiscuity, and poor academic performance. Such behavior is not what liberal educators had in mind when they introduced secular humanism as the prevailing philosophy of our schools, but it is certainly the result. How far must our country regress before they admit their error and return to the Judeo-Christian foundation upon which was built the greatest nation in the world?

Tourism, the largest industry in the state of Florida, has experienced a sharp decline because of recent violence against tourists. Reports of the murder of tourists have diverted numbers of foreigners from vacationing in Florida, and as a result, the state has lost billions of dollars in revenue. Why can't our elite ruling class realize that society must live by a standard moral code if it intends to survive?

A country's laws inevitably reflect the conscience of the people or of the dominant element among them, be that element religious or secularist. There is no such thing as a neutral society.[2]

Our country originally manifested a commitment to the Ten Commandments, but little by little our commitment to God's laws waned. It used to be wrong to abort a child. Today, to our national shame, that is no longer the case. Pro-life activists are looked on today as a nuisance to society as they struggle to raise the nation's conscience on behalf of the unborn, but if the battle for human life is lost, the premature death of the elderly, euthanasia, may be next.

It used to be wrong to take another person's life (except in war or as capital punishment for a heinous crime after a trial by jury). Today, however, from the proliferation of "death and dying" classes and literature, as well as the following that Dr. Jack Kevorkian has drawn in his assisted suicides, anyone can see that we are growing closer to the legalization of euthanasia.

Through organizations such as the Hemlock Society—whose founder Derek Humphry prompted his partner and wife to kill herself once it was discovered that she had cancer—the traditional view of the sanctity of life has been altered. In the Netherlands, where euthanasia has advanced at an alarming rate, pro-life doctors fear that their society is moving "very quickly from birth control to death control."[3]

The Irony of History—During World War II, Holland was the only occupied country whose doctors refused to participate in the German euthanasia program. Dutch physicians openly defied an order to treat only those patients who had a good chance of full recovery. They recognized that to comply with the order would have been the first step away from their duty to care for all patients. The German officer who gave that order was later executed for war crimes. Remarkably, during the entire German occupation of Holland, Dutch doctors never recommended nor participated in one euthanasia death. Commenting on this fact in his essay "The Humane

Holocaust," highly respected British journalist Malcolm Muggeridge wrote that it took only a few decades "to transform a war crime into an act of compassion."[4]

Pornography used to be wrong and immoral in America. Such material was formerly considered a sign of moral decadence, but today that has largely changed. A 1973 Supreme Court decision that protected this kind of literature under the free-speech laws allowed the production of these lascivious magazines, videos, even interactive pornographic computer programs to continue. Today pornography has become a $10-billion-a-year industry. Strong arguments are made, from the correlating skyrocketing increase in rape and child molestation, of the effects of pornography.

But the secular media, which often directs public policy, is for the most part silent against the porn industry. Yet millions of youth are subjected to material that can cause moral and physical damage because of pornography.

State agencies are finding occasions to control and oversee children's welfare to an alarming degree. In any healthy civilization, this responsibility has normally rested upon parents, who should have the intimate knowledge of their children's needs. Thousands of parents have been outraged by the state's intrusion into the lives of their children through radically explicit forms of sex education, the dispensing of contraceptives, and performing abortions on minors often without parental consent. In many of these cases, government has clearly overstepped its bounds.

When one looks at the no-fault divorce laws in our land, it is not surprising that today so many marriages are ended each

223

year. Divorce laws have made breaking what was once a sacred covenant almost as easy as renewing one's driver's license. Such laws neither support marriage as a God-created institution, nor do they contribute to society's well-being.

Stories about witches and witchcraft are finding their way into school curricula while any remnant of the Christian faith—Bible reading and prayer—is strictly monitored, and in many cases barred altogether.

Secularism illustrates one of the most basic principles of Scripture: We reap what we sow. If we sow license and godlessness, we will reap more of the same. Our nation is reaping a bitter harvest of drug addiction, violent crime, thievery, and rape because we have sown sensuality and irresponsibility in our schools, our media, and even our entertainment.

AMERICA'S CULTURAL WAR IS A RELIGIOUS WAR

The war for our culture is a spiritual war. This is no simple controversy among Protestants, Catholics, and Jews; it is a war between two religious beliefs. The secularists who control education, government, media, and entertainment are on one side, and all those who know and worship the true God are on the other.

Americans need to learn that secularism produces moral and civil chaos, which in the past has been "resolved" by a dictator who forcibly restores order. This was the story in France, the motherland of modern skepticism and Enlightenment—humanism. Today secularism is mixed with German rationalism, Unitarianism, and socialism—a lethal mix. Although the secularizers only make up 20 to 25 percent of the population, they have gained more influence on our culture than the religious majority has.

It is time that Christians do their part to promote again the constitutional concept of religious liberty—which applies to Christians and non-Christians alike—and be the much-needed "salt and light" for the world. For example, in the domain of education, all people would benefit if biblical morality were taught. As the Bible says, "Righteousness exalts a nation, but sin is a disgrace to any people" (Prov. 14:34).

The secular media, the ACLU, People for the American Way, and other secularists contend that the most dangerous people in America are religious fundamentalists who would like to take us back into the "dark ages." They seem to have more respect for pornographers, pedophiles, homosexuals, and atheists than for the "religious right." Despite the excessive behavior of some Christians, religious people are not, or should not appear to be, a danger to law-abiding, morally minded people.

WILL THE SECULARISTS PREVAIL IN THE TWENTY-FIRST CENTURY?

The answer to the question of whether the secularist minority will continue to dominate in years to come depends on how Christians respond. If we sit back and do nothing, the religion of humanism will continue to dominate, and our land will continue its moral decline.

To paraphrase Edmund Burke, all that is necessary for the triumph of evil is for good men to do nothing. If, however, we realize that our freedom to preach the gospel and nurture the next generation is in critical danger, we may be motivated to get involved in society as "salt and light."

Some evangelicals say, "Our job is not to reclaim our culture but to win souls and advance the kingdom." What they don't seem to understand, however, is that if our culture is lost, our freedom to preach the gospel will also be lost. As we preach and teach the gospel, we must also be a voice in the marketplace of ideas. We must resist, for "like a trampled spring and a polluted well is a righteous man who gives way before the wicked" (Prov. 25:26).

Our primary responsibility as Christians *is* to win souls, build our churches, send out missionaries, and do whatever we can to advance the kingdom of our Lord. That is our first and primary calling and commitment. At the same time, we are also citizens of this world. Just as our heavenly citizenship exacts certain demands of us, so does our earthly citizenship. We see in Romans 13 and 1 Timothy 2 that we are to be in submission and pray for our leaders, for they are "ministers of God." But because of our unique freedom in America, unknown in New Testament days, we can also go to the polls and vote out of office those who do not share our respect for traditional moral values.

WHY DO SO MANY AMORAL PEOPLE GET ELECTED?

Ethics violations in the federal government, from the White House to the houses of Congress, seem to be proliferating. How do these amoral people get elected? Why does a nation of predominantly family-oriented people elect such anti-moral, antifamily liberals to represent them in government? There are many reasons, chief among which is the immeasurable influence of the liberal media, which protects liberals and castigates conservatives. During the past sixty or so years, liberals have exercised great influence over Congress, to some extent the White House, and over many of the local and state elective offices because of a liberal-dominated media.

If we had a neutral media, our government would be run by more religious, respectful, and morally committed officials. Their presence in office would be reflected in our laws and public policy. Instead, the mainline media attacks all conservatives, especially Christians, and distorts their policies and beliefs so that the local population is afraid to vote for them. They are often portrayed as bigoted or "right-wing fascists." Consequently, at election time, people are influenced to vote for liberals, believing they are compassionate moderates. Once their candidates get in office, naive voters are perplexed by the fact that they are misrepresented by those they elected.

Another reason so few Christians or traditional values people are elected is because so few Christians vote. For example, only 48 percent of the evangelicals—who have the most to lose by the election of liberals to office—voted in the 1992 presidential elections. A shocking 52 percent stayed home. In 1986 the percentage was even worse! Five conservative senators lost their races that year by a total of fifty-seven thousands votes, while 5 million Christians who voted in 1984 didn't bother to vote in 1986! As a result, control of the Senate passed to liberals.

It is time Christians realize that we have sufficient numbers to turn the political tide. With God's help, we can make the difference in the elections of the next decade. The big question is *will we?* Will we get out to vote on election day? If only 20 percent more of us would vote during the next decade, we could see a moral conscience return to government policy and government legislation. Unless this happens, we will continue to lose our standards of morality and righteousness as our conscience disappears altogether. If we don't exercise our rights and vote, we forfeit the chance to change our government and country peacefully.

VOTE ACCORDING TO MORALS, NOT PARTY AFFILIATION

Responsible Christian voting is no longer a matter of politics. It has become a matter of moral and cultural survival. We cannot tell you to go out and vote for all Republicans, for some of them are as liberal as their Democrat opponents. Morality is the issue! We are being destroyed internally by moral decay—the same way Rome was destroyed. If we are to save our country from moral self-destruction, we must elect candidates who share our moral commitment whenever possible, or at least those who come closest to doing so.

You must be careful, however, for liberal politicians will say anything they think you want to hear to secure your vote. Amid our well recognized moral crises, it is not uncommon to hear many liberals who *talk* about "moral values" but vote against every moral value that comes before them. It is important that you vote for a candidate who not only talks about moral values but works to promote them. Tim remembers campaigning for Senator Roger Jepsen back in 1984. Jepsen's opponent was Congressman Tom Harkin who was falling behind in the polls because of his strong position in favor of abortion. Actually as a congressman he had voted for abortion and abortion funding twenty-nine times. To counteract his growing pro-death image, he announced that he was "pro-life," blanketed the state with his rhetoric, and defeated Jepsen by half a percentage point. After his election, it was reported that when confronted with this fact, he laughed and said, "I *am* pro-life. I am against nuclear weapons. What could be more pro-life than that?" Since being in the Senate, Harkin has a voting record that makes him one of the most liberal voters in the Senate.

Voters can't always trust what politicians say. As John Locke once said, "The actions of men are the best interpreters of their thoughts." The best way to judge politicians is to evaluate how they vote on moral values and how committed they are to them.

MORAL MINIMUMS FOR THE CHRISTIAN VOTE

1. *Pro-life:* Christians should vote for the candidate most committed to promoting the life of the unborn and most strongly opposed to government funding of abortion. Believe it or not, polls show that most Americans oppose abortion for convenience or birth control. So should our elected officials!

2. *Decency in Literature:* The politician who does not oppose pornography and its spread does not deserve the Christian vote. It is a distortion of the First Amendment to claim constitutional protection of pornography.

3. *Family values:* It is all but impossible to separate "moral" values from "family" values, for they are very much interrelated. That which is moral is good for the family. Moreover, the family is the principal source for the transmission of moral values. Consequently, even the definition of family—a mar-

ried man and woman living together with their children by birth or adoption—should be protected by law. Therefore, the candidate who best supports the family deserves your vote. The following are pro-family measures politicians should support:

- The right of parents to decide what's best for their children. Legislators who vote to give government or government-approved agencies such as Planned Parenthood the power to determine whether children will be subjected to radically explicit sex education classes, as well as whether they'll be given condoms and abortion counseling, do not deserve your vote.
- Higher tax deductions for children so mothers can remain at home during the years in which their children are young.
- School choice without government intervention should be available to taxpayers in the form of vouchers to be cashed at the school that best reflects the values of the parents. The politician who doesn't understand that does not deserve your vote.

4. *Recognition of homosexuality as abnormal:* While most Christians feel compassion for homosexuals and sincerely desire that they receive Jesus Christ as their Lord and Savior and experience liberation from their lifestyle, we oppose any legislation that ignores the threat their high-risk sexual behavior poses to us and the entire community—particularly our young who may be vulnerable to that behavior during their impressionable years.

5. *Commitment to integrity:* Citizens should be expected to honor their parents, not commit murder, not commit

adultery, not bear false witness, and not covet. Man's personal relationship to God is a private matter, but candidates who are committed to the high moral values in their political philosophy, voting record, and personal life are worthy of the vote of the Christian community.

THE CHURCH MUST GET SERIOUS ABOUT SIN

We cannot speak for Catholics, Jews, and others who hold a theistic faith, but we can speak for Protestants. We have been Christians and active in churches for fifty years. It pains us to say that Christians do not always live out their own beliefs about the Scriptures.

The Lord Jesus Christ has called his church to holiness. The Christian is called to live by high standards. Recent surveys indicate that the conduct of the church isn't too different from that of the world. George Barna has assessed the state of Christianity in the nation:

> *Most Americans—about four out of five—describe themselves as "Christian." Some equate the term with a general belief in God. Still others say it has to do with religious practices such as attending church or "being religious." . . . Much of the spiritual dimension of the concept has been lost while the population has been immunized to the Christian faith.*
>
> *There is an interesting contradiction, too, between what most of us say we believe and what we do (or don't do) in response to those beliefs.[5]*

It is time that religious people became serious about holy living. For example, many of the filthy television shows that are corrupting the minds of the secularized society are being watched in Christian homes. Two or three hours in church on the weekend will not lessen the twenty or more hours of pollution viewed during the week. To renew our national conscience, people of all faiths are going to have to purify their minds and live their beliefs.

One of the basic teachings of the church used to be personal sanctification and separation from the world. The Bible states it clearly:

> *Do you not know that your bodies are members of Christ? Shall I then take away the members of Christ and make them members of a harlot? May it never be! Or do you not know that the one who joins himself to a harlot is one body with her? For He says, "The two will become one flesh." But the one who joins himself to the Lord is one spirit with Him. Flee immorality. Every other sin that a man commits is outside the body, but the immoral man sins against his own body. Or do you not know that your body is a temple of the Holy Spirit who is in you, whom you have from God, and that you are not your own? For you have been bought with a price: therefore glorify God in your body. (1 Cor. 6:15-20)*

Christians must be brought back to righteous conduct in the home, the marketplace, and the workplace. We can hardly expect secular citizens or others who do not take their faith seriously enough to live morally if we do not do so ourselves.

232

BOYCOTT SLEAZY ADVERTISERS

Another way we can get serious about restoring our national conscience is to stop patronizing those who sell or advertise that which is immoral. Almost all religious people (and many moral nonreligious individuals) recognize that pornography is harmful to any society. ACLU lawyers sold the Supreme Court the felonious idea that the First Amendment gives pornographers the right to produce and market sleazy filth. But freedom is not an absolute right; it comes with responsibilities. Legalizing pornography has produced an industry that has morally degraded our culture and many individuals as well.

Can you imagine what would happen in six months if all the religious people in our country politely informed store proprietors who sell such materials that they would take their shopping elsewhere? Pornography producers would definitely feel the impact.

Such a concerted program, if proclaimed from the pulpits and over Christian radio and television and in the religious magazines, would eventually motivate the people in the pews to get serious enough about moral indecency in our communities that we would stop subsidizing it. The same could be done with advertisers of products who subsidize morally degrading films and television shows by sponsoring them.

The serious threat of a boycott by Christians would certainly cause producers to think twice about advertising on immoral, antifamily programs. The problem is, we religious-minded people are just not serious enough about morality. If we were, we would stop patronizing those who contribute to the moral destruction of society. It is one thing to look at the moral devastation surrounding us and deplore it as if we could do nothing to halt the moral hemorrhaging of our society. It is quite another to get serious and do something about it.

THE ENTERTAINMENT INDUSTRY NEEDS TO BE CLEANED UP

We have already seen that the entertainment industry has more influence on the moral climate of our country than the church or any other agency. There is no possibility that it will clean itself up *unless it is forced to do so!* The people who make up that industry don't seem to understand how morally degrading and harmful their programs are.

The religious people in this country need to send a message the entertainment industry will understand by patronizing only those movies and watching only those television programs and buying only those music albums that do not flaunt or promote immorality. Ted Baehr has found that most Christians watch the same television programs and see the same movies as non-Christians, only sometimes adding to that media diet a dose of religious programs. Baehr writes:

> *The overwhelming majority of the Christians in the United States have the same media habits as the non-Christian population! If Christians would redirect their entertainment dollars away from immoral entertainment toward moral movies, producers would take notice and produce movies and programs for us.*[6]

If television and movie producers cannot produce forms of entertainment that adhere to at least a minimum standard of decency, we should not patronize them. Their numbers are not sufficient to subsidize their enormous production budgets, so they would be forced to produce a product that caters to the consumer. The religious and morally minded citizens in this nation could even bring cable companies—many of which have abandoned all pretense of moral decency—to reverse course.

AMERICA NEEDS A MORAL TELEVISION NETWORK

One of the things a few wealthy individuals with strong religious values could do for America would be to invest some of their wealth in buying production studios to produce programming committed to traditional moral values. We believe gifts to some high-quality production companies using morally committed individuals could produce programming that would not only have a wholesome influence on our country but also inspire some of the present programmers to clean up their act.

We have already observed that the entertainment industry has done more to destroy moral values in this country than anything else, yet the government has allowed them to use the so-called government-controlled airwaves—both radio and television—to do it. The entertainment industry continually tests the limits of the Federal Communications Commission (FCC), the government "watchdog" to regulate the industry. A 1963 House of Representatives report on the FCC set forth the philosophy underlying the Communications Act that founded the FCC:

235

Under our system, the interests of the public are dominant. The commercial needs of licensed broadcasters and advertisers must be integrated into those of the public. Hence, individual citizens and the communities they compose owe a duty to themselves and their peers to take an active part in the scope and quality of the television service which . . . has a vast impact on their lives and on the lives of their children. . . . They are the owners of the channels of television—indeed of all broadcasting.[7]

Unfortunately, the FCC does not always remember that we, the public, are the owners of television. Every year more nudity, profanity, violence, and immorality are allowed on the "federally controlled airwaves." Occasionally the FCC will file a complaint, but more often than not, they are derelict in their responsibilities. The latest American Family Association (AFA) report states that during a period of one year during prime time, the three major networks aired approximately 30,030 sex, violence, and profanity incidents. A total of 84 percent of all sex was depicted outside of marriage.[8]

It is obvious that someone hasn't been protecting the interests of society from the moral perverts' use of the airwaves to portray adultery, fornication, homosexuality, and nudity. The government is not demanding that moral standards of community decency be adhered to in programming.

Most people are unaware that it would be very simple for the FCC to solve the problem. Every three years stations are up for license renewal. If our government were not so dominated by secularists, it would set a moral standard based on the traditional values this country was founded on and threaten to refuse to renew the license of any station that did not maintain a high moral standard in its programming.

Stations do not own their frequency—they just think they do. They are leased at the option of the FCC. Obviously then, the smut and filth on television, cable, and radio are controllable by the government. For several years government has abdicated its responsibility, and consequently, the industry is morally out of control. An FCC whose members took seriously their responsibilities could solve the problem in a short period of time, but such action would require support from the president, the Justice Department, and the federal courts. Obviously, these government agencies have been controlled by secularizers who let the FCC operate the way it does because they approve of the moral degradation that continually floods the airwaves.

Many young people pick up their moral values from music, television, and the movies, but today's media pays little or no attention to America's time-honored traditional values. "Sex sells," and consequently the media goes with what sells. Since they see that religious people are a threat to their control, they do their best to belittle, distort, and ignore them.

Why doesn't television programming highlight some of the many people whose achievements are noteworthy? In flipping through the television fare one night, we were confronted with *Murphy Brown* and two other comedies making fun of unwed women who got pregnant. This is hardly the type of person most parents would like to see their children emulate.

If the media is the most powerful force in our culture today, then they should start policing their morals so they can make a contribution for good to our society. It is interesting to me that the secularizers bend over backward in our federally controlled schools to keep atheists from being offended by the mention of God, prayer, or morality, yet over the federally controlled airwaves Christians can be offended every day of the week by the broadcasting of blasphemy against God and the Lord Jesus Christ or attacks on our moral values. It is time "the fairness doctrine" was applied for Christians as well. After all, we are citizens and pay 38 percent of our nation's taxes! And there are probably another 38 percent who share our moral yearnings for our culture.

In a free society there will always be those who commit immoral acts, but such things are usually done in secret. Making them public, by filming these events and putting them into the homes of 250 million people, doesn't mean such behavior is right. During the past fifty years the media has abused its freedoms and by its irresponsibility has hastened the moral chaos in our country.

GOVERNMENT SHOULD PROTECT FAMILIES

The strength of a nation lies in its families, and certain government programs are becoming enemies of Christian families. Instead of protecting families, it has tried to change even the definition of *family.* One of the first things government could do is to raise the tax exemption for children to enable more families to go back to a single breadwinner, leaving the other parent at home for the sake of the children.

One of the greatest social problems we have in this country is teenage pregnancy. Sixty-six percent of inner-city babies are born into fatherless homes to unwed mothers, and our government subsidizes the behavior by offering financial support to these unwed mothers. Some are reported to purposely get pregnant as a means of increasing the size of their welfare and Aid to Dependent Children checks. Welfare payments should be tied to education or work or both—otherwise we will make some women dependent on welfare for life. Government officials seem to take the attitude that chastity is an impossible goal. If 51 percent of the girls and 63 percent of the boys are sexually active by the time they graduate from high school, that means that 49 percent of the girls and 37 percent of the boys are virgins when they complete twelfth grade. And that is with no government encouragement at all. A recent survey by *USA Today* indicates that "seven out of ten adults and teens back the message of abstinence before marriage and 44 percent think young people hear too little about virtue until marriage."[9] If our government was morally responsible, they would lead our nation's youth in a high-level campaign for virtue till marriage—instead of giving them unsafe condoms.

EDUCATION MUST BECOME RESPONSIVE TO PARENTS AND TAXPAYERS

Free enterprise is the economic marvel of the world because it thrives on competition. The old Soviet Union should forever be an example that government monopoly and interference with business stultifies the economy. In this country we determined long ago that monopolies were harmful to the country.

Education (our public school system), the biggest monopoly in our country, is failing in its job, even with $500 billion of taxpayers' money every year. Academic levels—reading ability in particular—have gone down in direct proportion to the increase in budget and stultifying control by the Federal Education Department. The voucher system, mentioned earlier in the book, letting parents take a school voucher to the school they choose, would suddenly put an end to the education monopoly and make education competitive, which in turn would improve academic quality.

Religious People Must Teach Values to Their Children

We cannot trust secularists to teach morality, respect for God and parents, or the values Christians agree are good and wholesome. Parents will have to take more seriously their responsibility for such moral training.

At a time when our culture acts like it has none, Christian parents should accept the responsibility of strengthening their children's conscience by the teaching of the Word of God in the home. Six thousand Christian bookstores in this country sell wholesome books, tapes, videos, and other materials that will help you train your young. Children are going to watch or hear something. Why shouldn't we spend some money and help them learn that which is going to give them principles to live by?

We cannot allow the consciences of our nation's children to suffer because of our neglect. We hope America will begin to take steps to renew her conscience, for there is much to be gained in our future.

there is hope for america

....

10

As a nation, we have squandered the blessings of God and the legacy of our Christian forefathers' prayers. When we show more concern for ice-trapped whales and snail darters than we do for our unborn babies, we deserve anything but God's blessing. We condemn the innocent and pardon the guilty. We have forgotten the pledges and vows of our forefathers in our quest for convenience and comfort.

Many people in the Lord's work have given up on the future of America. Some even see in our present moral decadence a fulfillment of the prophecy found in 2 Timothy 3:1-6:

> *In the last days difficult times will come. For men will be lovers of self, lovers of money, boastful, arrogant, revilers, disobedient to parents, ungrateful, unholy, unloving, irreconcilable, malicious gossips, without self-control, brutal, haters of good, treacherous, reckless, conceited, lovers of pleasure rather than lovers of God; holding to a form of godliness, although they have denied its power; and avoid such men as these. For among them are those who enter into households and captivate weak women weighed down with sins, led on by various impulses.*

Who could deny that our decaying culture mirrors this prediction of the last days? In his recent book *The Vanishing Conscience,* a clarion call for Christians and the church to return to a biblical conscience, our friend John MacArthur shares his feelings about the seemingly hopeless situation of America today:

> *"Reclaiming" the culture is a pointless, futile exercise. I am convinced we are living in a post-Christian society—a civilization that exists under God's judgment. . . . Abundant evidence suggests that God has given this culture over to its own depravity. Certainly He is not interested in moral reform*

242

*for an unregenerate society. God's purpose in this world—and
the church's only legitimate commission—is the proclamation
of the message of sin and salvation to individuals, whom God
sovereignly redeems and calls out of the world. God's purpose
is to save those who will repent of their sins and believe the
gospel—not to work for external corrections in a morally
bankrupt culture.*[1]

Personally, we have serious problems with that kind of
thinking. No one knows for certain whether these are indeed
the last days. Being a teacher of Bible prophecy, Tim is
inclined to agree that we may indeed be in the last days, but
the Bible is not specific, and we may be a hundred or more
years away from the last days. No one really knows.

Consequently, instead of just waiting for the Rapture to
take all Christians up to the Father's house, we must realize
that Christ may not return until the end of the next century.
If we just give up on our country, America may be sentenced
to an unnecessary hundred or so years living without the
freedom to preach the gospel here or around the world—simply because we gave up on our culture too soon. America may
be, as John suggests, "a civilization that exists under God's
judgment." The question is, Will God judge a nation like
ours because secularists have seized the agencies of greatest
influence and are using them to move the majority of family-
oriented people toward Sodom and Gomorrah? We think not!

We are convinced that this country and the freedom and
opportunity it still provides to preach the gospel around the
world are worth fighting for. Besides, that is our duty as
responsible Christian citizens. The same Lord who challenged

us to be "the light of the world" also challenged us to be "the salt of the earth." We refuse to give this country over to the secularists without a fight—and we are convinced there are millions of other Christians who share our concern.

THE CHURCH'S RESTRAINING INFLUENCE ON SOCIETY

For two thousand years the church has been a "restraining" influence on society. During the first three centuries the gospel was so widely spread that it reached the emperor of Rome. In A.D. 312, Constantine publicized his personal faith and made Christianity a legal religion. Not until Satan sowed the false teachings of allegorizing Scripture did the church embrace pagan religious rites and practices that today can only be labeled "barbaric"—for instance the Inquisition and the slaughter of the French Huguenots.

The spread of the Protestant Reformation throughout Europe and Germany brought civility into formerly barbaric countries. Wherever Christianity has spread, there has been an attempt to establish the Ten Commandments as the basis of social order. That certainly was the case in the founding of America.

As we have seen, the "natural law" of human conscience was the basis of this country's social and public conduct for more than three hundred years. Businesses shut down in respect for God and his day of worship. Family and marriage values were regarded as sacred, and the church did not hesitate to direct its "public servants" to reject any deviant laws or trends.

Not until secular influences began to have more effect than religious influences did our nation move away from moral foundations based on absolute truths of the Scripture. But as secularism began to influence public education, the print and wire media, and the entertainment industry, the results began to show up in the kind of people who were elected to hold public office. Public morality today reflects these changes. All the while, the church was either passive or unwilling to face the challenge of the onslaught of downward trends in morality.

The church's primary mandate, of course, has always been the Great Commission. The church neglects her soul-winning directive at her peril. And while we are not a perfect church, since World War II we have been far more faithful to our first command to spread the "light of the world" than we have to being the salt of the earth.

Yet all these soul-winning activities have not been a restraining influence on our society. In fact, while the number of souls coming to Christ has gone up and Bible-teaching churches have increased in size and number, the moral level of our culture has gone down. Why? Because the church has not obeyed our second mandate of being the "restraining" influence on society as the salt of the earth. I am inclined to believe that if our Lord were to address Christian leaders today, he would speak to them as he did to the scribes and Pharisees on the subject of tithing: "these [soul winning] are the things you should have done without neglecting the others" (Matt. 23:23).

THE CHURCH'S ROLE IN THE LAST DAYS

The role of the church in the end times is not obscure in prophecy. She is seen as the agency through which the Holy Spirit "restrains" society in the last days. In 2 Thessalonians 2:7

we read of those days prior to the appearance of "the man of lawlessness" who will eventually lead the world into a head-long rejection of God and his moral absolutes. The passage says that "he who now restrains will do so until he is taken out of the way." Most Bible scholars believe this is a reference to the Holy Spirit as he indwells the church and leads her to be a "restraining" force in the world in which we live.

Christians are having an impact today when they refuse to spend their money in stores that sell pornography, or buy products from companies who sponsor immoral programs on television, or inform the advertisers of their displeasure with the type of programs they are promoting. We all have opportunities every day for doing restraining work as we are led and empowered by the Holy Spirit. We are convinced that if the church in our country will begin to take seriously her responsibility of being that restraining influence, we can still turn this nation back to God.

A recent illustration is the Dallas, Texas, group of Christians who became disillusioned with the secularist and anti-moral policies of their school district. Instead of giving up, they recruited three members to run for the school board, got out the church vote on election day, and elected them all—one by only seventeen votes! (See how important your vote can be?) Now Christian traditional values thinkers outnumber the secularizers on that board three to two. Would to God this could happen all over America.

OUR OPTIMISM ABOUT AMERICA'S FUTURE
At the risk of alienating some of our less-optimistic brethren, we still believe God has a plan for this nation's

future. There are four reasons for our optimism. Please weigh them carefully.

1. *God is a merciful God.* Even the rebellious prophet Jonah knew God was merciful, for he said, "I knew that you are a gracious and compassionate God, slow to anger and abounding in love, a God who relents from sending calamity" (Jon. 4:2, NIV). If God had dealt with this country on the basis of what we deserve, we would have ceased to be a nation long ago.

The place where we more seriously take issue with those who forecast gloom, doom, and despair for the future of America is the subject of whom God holds accountable for the sins of this country. Will God judge the 250 million citizens of our land or those who have indoctrinated and educated people, leaving them with the kind of moral values they hold—those in the entertainment industry, education, media, and government? In the eyes of God, who is most deserving of his judgment—the evil shepherds or the sheep they are leading astray?

We still believe that even as morally dark as America is today, we could yet experience a moral, spiritual revival—not because we deserve it, but because God is a merciful God, abundant in loving-kindness. Just as he spared the wicked city of Nineveh in the days of the prophet Jonah, so he may yet spare America. As God himself said, "And should I not have compassion on Nineveh, the great city in which there are more than 120,000 persons who do not know the difference between their right and left hand, as well as many animals?" (Jon. 4:11).

If God would save Nineveh because of 120,000 innocent

boys and girls, "who didn't know their left hand from their right," why would he not also save America? We have 45 million children, many of whom "don't know their right hand from their left" or don't know right from wrong because they have been brainwashed by secularists who taught them "there are no moral absolutes."

We believe that our merciful God will yet spare America because of who and what he is. But there is another reason, a principle of his Word that he has honored for over 3,500 years.

2. *The Abrahamic covenant!* Many believe that God will save America because of his promise to Abraham made thousands of years ago. God performed a biological miracle on the bodies of Abraham and Sarah, and created a new nation of people called the Hebrews, or the Jews. A part of God's promise was to "make you a great nation, and I will bless you, and make your name great; and so you shall be a blessing; and *I will bless those who bless you,* and *the one who curses you I will curse.* And in you all the families of the earth shall be blessed" (Gen. 12:2-3, emphasis added).

In our opinion, one of our nation's most worthwhile accomplishments has been its consistent regard for the plight of the Jewish nation. During the eighteenth century, in both England and the United States, a more detailed interpretation of Bible prophecy arose that was called premillennialism. Premillennialists believe that the return of Christ will occur before the Millennium, a position held by most evangelicals today. As a result of the Reformation, the Bible was taken out of the dark ages and translated for the common people. This caused them to take a closer look at the Scriptures referring to the millennial period, which they interpreted literally. Consequently, Christians began to see that a future restoration of the nation of Israel was part of the prophetic teachings of Scripture. Gradually they began to recognize that God was not through with the Jewish nation and that there would be a regathering of the nation of Israel. As early as the middle of the eighteenth century, Christian groups began calling for the restoration of the Jews to their biblical homeland—Palestine.

Jews were soon welcomed to New York and other cities in America where they were treated to unprecedented freedom. They had a significant part in the industrial revolution of this country. Jews have enjoyed more freedom in America for a longer period of time than in any other major country since they were driven from their land centuries ago. Even England has not always been as charitable to the Jews as America. Some have been bold enough to say that the decline of the British Empire resulted from her mistreatment of the Jews or her accommodating policy toward the Arabs during the thirties and forties.

America has committed many sins, for which we may well deserve judgment, but as a nation we have been a consistent friend of the Jews and the nation of Israel.

Many nations that have been evil to the Jews have suffered for it. Some may claim that this fact is simply a coincidence, but others see a clearer purpose of God in it. England has already been mentioned, but before them there was France, Spain, Italy, and the list goes on. In very recent times, the Soviet Union collapsed under its own weight after many years of mistreatment of the Jews.

America, by contrast, has been one of the major benefactors of the Jews. In 1948 President Harry Truman helped persuade the United Nations to recognize the nation of Israel. Since then, we have contributed more than $50 billion of foreign aid to that state of more than 4 million people. Without our protection, the nation of Israel would probably not exist today.

3. *The strong hand of Providence in America.* God will spare America because, as the framers of our Constitution believed, his hand was on the founding of our nation. Anyone familiar with the history of this country knows that it is a miracle nation. Without "the strong hand of Providence," as George Washington called it, we would never have survived in the first place. Among this country's first settlers were Christian Pilgrims who claimed they would never have made it through that first long, cold winter without divine intervention.

Recently, we took our granddaughter to the site on the Delaware River where God supernaturally arranged a fog through which General Washington was able to lead seven thousand troops and eighteen hundred wounded soldiers to safety during a British siege that would have effectively destroyed any chance of winning the Revolutionary War. Our fledgling country's victory was a miracle, as was victory in the War of 1812—and the list goes on. God had a plan in founding this nation, and a great part of his plan, no doubt, involved using the United States as a beacon and bearer of the gospel. No other country has so cooperated with God's worldwide plan of getting the gospel to people of "every tribe and tongue and people and nation" (Rev. 5:9).

Politically, America has been an inspiration to freedom-loving people throughout the earth. Without it, the world would be enslaved today by either Adolph Hitler or godless communism.

We believe that America has yet to fulfill her destiny. In order that we may, God will send us one more great revival as he has done at least three times before. It is our prayer, however, that we will also have legislative reform to enable the revival to become long lasting. Otherwise, a revival will be short-lived. Liberal secularists have legislated immorality into our culture; it must be overturned by legislation in order to restore traditional moral values in the public square. That will require about 30 percent more elected officials committed to such values during the next thirty to fifty years.

4. *More Christians in America than any country on earth.* During God's conversation with Abraham, found in Genesis 18, God agreed to spare Sodom and Gomorrah if he could find within ten righteous souls. As you recall, ten could not be found. And while we are not blind to the glaring evils of our nation, there is no other major country on earth with as many Spirit-filled, Bible-believing Christians. Gallup polls tell us that 60 to 70 million of us claim to have been "born again." Frankly, could it be that this 60 to 70 million may be what is preserving America from God's destruction today? The judging hand of God has never fallen on any nation in history that had the percentage of Christians that this nation possesses. Consequently, we do not think God will destroy America, but we might expect him to discipline her. Nations, like many individuals, can rarely be trusted with great blessing. The "good life" in America is not conducive to faith in God. In the Old Testament, the nation of Israel had that same problem—that is why they went through the cycles found in

the book of Judges. They strayed from God and his moral values, and God sent a nation to humble them and bring them back to him. Time after time God heard their cry and sent them a deliverer.

America may even now be experiencing the judgment of God, for certainly we are faced with disasters of all sorts. We have already seen the plagues of AIDS and other sexually transmitted diseases. Our nation has experienced the worst two years of natural phenomena in history, with devastating hurricanes in Florida, floods in the Midwest, deadly blizzards in the northeast, and earthquakes in southern California. Add to that riots, our unprecedented crime wave, and the ever-present threat of nuclear proliferation and terrorism. No one can say with certainty that these problems *are* definitely God's judgment, but neither can anyone say with certainty that some of them are not!

Our question to our doomsayer friends who think the U.S. ship of state is about to be sunk like the *Titanic* in the sea by her own depravity is, *Would a merciful God who has announced his plan to reach the entire world with the gospel before the end of the age destroy a nation that is doing as much as America to accomplish his purposes?* We think not!

God could, of course, for he is sovereign and can raise up whom he chooses to do his will. Besides, we have no certainty that we are close to the end of the age. Some fear that God may already be turning eastward, to countries such as Korea, where Christianity and Christian mission work have been growing exponentially.

While we may be living in a post–Christian culture at

the present time, we should not allow ourselves to limit God. Instead, we should expect him, one way or another, to bring glory to himself, perhaps through giving us one more chance for a revival that will return this nation to moral sanity by reestablishing the moral traditions we once held. The revival of our nation will not be automatic, nor will it take place unless the church begins to dedicate itself to its full mandate to act as salt and light to our needy society.

WHAT THE CHURCH CAN DO TO HELP SAVE AMERICA

Rescue those being led away to death; hold back those staggering toward slaughter. If you say, "But we knew nothing about this," does not he who weighs the heart perceive it? (Prov. 24:11-12, NIV)

This book was written during the year *Schindler's List* became a box office smash hit and won two Oscars for Steven Spielberg, so it's only natural that we think of the Holocaust as the ultimate expression of man's inhumanity to man. But the secularist philosophies of Adolph Hitler, Mao Tse-tung, Joseph Stalin, and other dictators have led to the cruel murder of more than 170 million men, women, and children in this century. To the secularist, human life is expendable. He has rights without responsibilities.

That philosophy found its ultimate expression in German National Socialism, the political party that massacred at least 17 million people (including 6 million Jews) and instigated World War II. The death mask of secularism that produced the Third Reich was not the most terrible situation during that tragic time. To us, the most painful situation in all of Germany was the silence of the church at a time of moral crisis. We would assume most of the leaders of the church disagreed with Hitler's plans for the Jews, but for the most part they did not oppose him. In fact, in some cases they even helped him!

Erwin Lutzer tells the following pathetic story:

> Let us not forget that in Germany during the late thirties the church initially took a neutral political position as Hitler came to power with his plans for war and the extermination of the Jews. Later, that neutrality became acceptance of Hitler's agenda. The Lutheran church actually passed a resolution condemning Jews and excluding them from their worship services. The Christians had adopted Hitler's National Socialism as a part of their creed. Their spokesman, Herman Gruner, made clear what they stood for:
>
> "The time is fulfilled for the German people in Hitler. It is because of Hitler that Christ, God the helper and redeemer has become effective among us. Therefore National Socialism is positive Christianity in action. Hitler is the way of the Spirit and the will of God for the German people to enter the church of Christ."
>
> In September 1933 the church in much of Germany adopted the Aryan Clause, which denied the pulpit to ordained ministers of Jewish blood. But Dietrich Bonhoeffer protested, saying that the church should "jam the spokes of the wheel" of the state if the persecution of the Jews should continue. Many of the clergy became angry and although Bonhoeffer was able to obtain 2,000

signatures, to his disappointment the leaders of the church fell silent to his martyrdom.

Bonhoeffer's friend Martin Niemoller led a similar pastor's Emergency League that rejected the Aryan Clause. Eventually 6,000 pastors joined and became the nucleus of the "confessing church." Under orders by Hitler, Niemoller was imprisoned and later placed in solitary confinement. He was freed after the war, and whenever he concluded a speech he ended with the words that have now become famous:

"First, they came for the socialists, and I did not speak out because I was not a socialist. They then came for the trade unionists, and I did not speak out because I was not a trade unionist. Then they came for the Jews, and I did not speak out because I was not a Jew. Then they came for me, and there was no one left to speak out for me."[2]

Thank God we have many Christian leaders who have raised their voice in opposition to America's secularist movement, which would stifle all dissent in this country the way they have stifled dissent in the public schools. Christian leaders have been joined by courageous Catholics, as well as some conservative Jews and other religious leaders, in their observation of the dangers of the amoral culture infecting our nation.

Ever since our San Diego church was denied an application for approval to build a new auditorium, we have realized the importance of the Christian's responsibility to vote. The application was denied by six secularists who hated churches. That was in 1970, but since then we have seen similar illustrations of secularist discrimination that stymies the growth of churches all over the country. Right here in Virginia, we saw a fine church refused a building permit on seventy-six acres of land, just three miles from a music center that attracts enormous crowds and creates unbelievable traffic problems. The reason is simple. Secularizers approve wild rock concerts in their communities, but they disapprove of churches. We keep hoping such acts of governmental discrimination against Christians and churches will prompt pastors by the thousands to wake up and get their members out to vote on election day.

It isn't a matter of asking all Christians to become politically active, of which some of our critics accuse us. The real issue is responsible Christian citizenship. The Christian who doesn't vote has lost his right to complain about how the secularists run his community or country.

What the Church Cannot Do

The church must be reminded that it is not the master or the servant of the state, but rather the conscience of the state. It must be the guide and the critic of the state, and never its tool. If the church does not recapture its prophetic zeal, it will become an irrelevant social club without moral or spiritual authority.—Martin Luther King Jr.[3]

As the conscience of the state and under God, the church's first responsibilities are to preach the gospel, win souls, and build up the body of Christ. But we also have a God-given responsibility to lead our people not only to avoid the unfruitful works of darkness, but also expose them (see Eph. 5:11, NIV). If the ministers of America would fearlessly expose the unfruitful secularizers who control our culture and are leading it to Sodom and Gomorrah, we could turn this country around in one decade!

There are, however, a few limitations that must be placed on churches and ministers if they do not wish to lose their tax-exempt status.

1. Ministers and churches cannot officially endorse a candidate. Frankly, we don't think that would be wise in any circumstance. We preach a nonpartisan gospel; there are Christians from all parties at almost every church service. A minister can get involved in election activities as a private citizen apart from his church. And just because a candidate claims to be a Christian doesn't mean we should automatically vote for him.

The church is no place for promoting candidates. That can be done discreetly by mail or in personal visits. Congressman Duncan Hunter owes his twelve years in the U.S. Congress to Jim Baise, a young Baptist minister from National City, California, who decided that their liberal congressman had to go. Jim got six other pastors to help him, and as private citizens, they and their people canvassed their district. When the votes were counted, Hunter won by four thousand votes, and that district has enjoyed nearly 100 percent conservative voting representation in Congress for fourteen years. We need 150 more Jim Baises in this country!

And his church? It has nearly tripled its effectiveness in soul winning and ministry during these past fourteen years. The last time Tim preached for Jim's church, there were eighteen hundred people in his congregation.

People in this country are looking for men of God who

have enough guts to stand up and warn the church that moral barbarians are storming the gates. To accomplish that, pastors do not need to—nor should they—endorse candidates from the pulpit.

2. Pastors and churches should *never* collect money in the church or use church money to promote a candidate. The followers of Jesse Jackson can get by with that; on national television we saw them take offerings in churches for Jesse's 1988 run for the White House. The liberals in government and the media never objected or accused the pastors who supported him of doing anything illegal—though they most certainly were.

But pastors, as private citizens, can raise money *outside* the church and spend it for political activities—privately, like any other citizen—but never in the name of the church. Usually, however, a less visible friend will be glad to handle that to avoid the appearance of impropriety by the pastor.

3. Pastors *can* encourage the entire congregation to register to vote, inform them on the voting record of all the candidates and/or their position on moral issues, and lead in a "get-out-to-vote" campaign on election day.

While we were on the staff of one of the fastest-growing churches in the country, located in Dallas, Texas, we saw an example of responsible Christian citizenship in action that, if followed in every church, could easily return this nation to moral sanity. For weeks before the presidential election, we had voter registration available in the foyer of the church, and occasionally the pastor urged the members to become responsible citizens by registering to vote. Then on election day, all ten thousand members were called by telephone volunteers in the "Get out the vote" campaign to assure maximum participation. In the 1994 local elections, that pastor got his great church so involved in the "Get out the vote" campaign that three Christians won tightly contested school board seats— one by only seventeen votes. If that pastor had remained silent, the secularists would still control that school board. If every church had done that in 1992, Bill Clinton would still be governor of Arkansas.

4. Pastors *can* encourage the women of the church to organize a Concerned Women for America prayer-action chapter. The meeting could be announced in the weekly bulletin and scheduled to meet on a weekly or monthly basis. Some churches have opened their CWA chapters to couples, men and women. Other chapters meet on weekday mornings when it is convenient for mothers whose children are in school.

CWA sends out important educational information for parents and prayer-action alerts that are within the legal boundaries for a church. The national office of CWA would be glad to assist any church that is interested in this valuable ministry.

WHAT WE MUST DO: COMBINE OUR HOPE WITH ACTION

Unfortunately, far too many Christians remain silent in the face of moral chaos and impending doom. They may be concerned enough to express themselves privately, but their policy is never to mix politics and religion. Many of them are actually proud of their silence, either because they don't understand what the Bible says about being salt and light or because they were trained in seminary to believe that religion and politics don't mix. What they don't understand is that the secularizers themselves have politicized morality. In the good old days you could talk about abortion, prayer, and homosexuality without offending anyone's politics because these issues had *not been politicized!* But today you can't speak out on abortion, homosexual rights, gambling, pornography, or prayer in school without the liberals screaming that you're trying to legislate morality. Maybe they need to consider that we'd like to *legislate* it.

I had a discussion with a well-known Christian broadcaster about prominent Christian leaders and broadcasters who do and don't speak out on some of these political issues that affect the morality of our nation. We noted one in particular who would have great influence if he spoke out. Unfortunately, this person is still silent. If he spoke out, millions would follow. Frankly, I am ashamed of some of my minister colleagues who rarely use their God-given influence to take a stand for morality in the public square. Instead, they feel more comfortable remaining politically aloof in this morally depraved period of American history. That way they avoid being called "controversial."

In this day, my friend, the minister who isn't controversial, is too quiet. It is not possible today for a minister to preach the "whole counsel of God" as it appears in the Word without offending someone's politics. The secularizers' have politicized morality, and the politically correct line of our day is diametrically opposed to the Word of God on every important issue.

Incidentally, if you are blessed with a pastor who refuses to be intimidated by the "Nervous Nellies" of your congregation who call him every time he speaks out on an issue, be sure you call him and commend him for his courage. And if he is willing to lead the congregation in such controversial things as registering to vote at election time, (which is really just responsible Christian citizenship) be sure to volunteer to help and be encouraging.

And if you live in an area where the owner or manager of a Christian radio or television station speaks out from time to time on the moral issues of our day, be sure to write, phone, and financially support him. It is unbelievable to us, in view of the moral crisis that is destroying millions of our nation's youth every day, how many Christian radio or television station managers act as if we were still living in the fifties. They don't speak up and would jerk anyone off their station or network who did.

Tim remembers when he did a three-minute *Capitol Report* for radio and television that was carried on 250 stations. One day he mentioned a South Carolina senator who had introduced an extremely liberal piece of legislation that should be opposed by the Christian community. The next day the station manager received one lone telephone complaint from an elderly listener because someone spoke out "against our senator." So the next day he cancelled Tim's program from nineteen stations. So much for Christian courage in a time of moral crisis!

But he is not alone. One of our close pastor friends is so afraid of losing his tax-exempt status for his radio station that he refuses to carry *Beverly LaHaye Live,* Beverly's daily talk show from Washington, D.C., even though a few months

before she had won the National Religious Broadcasters'
award for "Talk Show Host of the Year."

It is about time Christian communicators of all kinds speak
out on the issues today. Like the prophet Ezekiel, we are to be
"watchmen" to our generation. A watchman does no good if
he just sits and watches the enemy approaching while doing
nothing to warn the people:

> *"But if the watchman sees the sword coming and does not*
> *blow the trumpet, and the people are not warned, and a*
> *sword comes and takes a person from them, he is taken*
> *away in his iniquity; but his blood I will require from the*
> *watchman's hand." Now as for you, son of man, I have*
> *appointed you a watchman for the house of Israel; so you*
> *will hear a message from My mouth, and give them*
> *warning from Me. When I say to the wicked, "O wicked*
> *man, you shall surely die," and you do not speak to warn*
> *the wicked from his way, that wicked man shall die in his*
> *iniquity, but his blood I will require from your hand.*
> *(Ezek. 33:6-8)*

We need watchmen who aren't afraid to speak out. Secularists don't hesitate to impose their speech or promote their
godless candidates on their networks or through their various
communication vehicles, but many in the Christian media
are intimidated into silence.

One of my minister friends gave me that old Christian
passivist bromide: "LaHaye, God didn't call me to save our
culture. He called me to preach the gospel." My response to
him was, "Thank God the preachers at the time of the

Revolutionary War didn't have that attitude. You wouldn't be enjoying the freedom you have today to preach the gospel."

For twenty-five years we pastored a wonderful church in San Diego, California. During that time Tim earned the title of being controversial because of his political activism. He wears that title as a badge of honor. It came because every time we had an election he would organize an ad hoc group of eighteen well-known ministers of the area and print their names on letterhead called "San Diego Council for Good Government." After his committee interviewed candidates, they endorsed those with the clearest commitment to the moral values in which they believed. They never endorsed candidates through their churches, nor did they fund them with church money. Instead they raised money privately and sent letters to the ministers of the city who privately distributed them at their discretion. Consequently, all five representatives from that part of California are conservatives with strong voting records on the moral issues.

Tim's activities may have been considered controversial to People for the American Way and other leftist secularizers, but he acted within his rights and responsibilities as a citizen concerned for the welfare of our country and our state. And it certainly didn't hurt the soul-winning endeavors or growth of our church, which grew ten times larger during our twenty-five years there. Actually, his activism combined with his soul winning and practical Bible teaching enhanced the church's growth.

We want to see moral values returned as the official public policy of our land and to guarantee the perpetuation of religious freedom for all churches and synagogues.

The secularizers want to profit financially by the sale of smut and sleaze on television or video or in print—regardless of how many people are injured, killed, or offended. If Christians and their ministers are too afraid of being considered controversial to raise their voice in warning and encourage Christians to become responsible voting citizens at election time, they will eventually preside over the death of Christianity in this country.

We may already be too late. But if we are, we would rather stand at the funeral of our country knowing we did our best to save it than wish we had been better watchmen on the wall.

If Rationalism wishes to govern the world without regard to the religious needs of the soul, the experience of the French Revolution is there to teach us the consequences of such a blunder.—Joseph Renan, 1866 [4]

our
conscience:

11

Every day we live with the results of secularists who are actively transforming our nation's culture and values via government, education, the media, the entertainment industry, and almost every other conceivable sphere of influence in society. These spheres are not evil in themselves, but rather the value systems of those who control and operate them are flawed. Consequently, they inevitably produce socially destructive effects.

This nation's loss of conscience is directly proportional to the secularizing policies of those who have usurped control of it and changed it. As you know, our Constitution was founded by a predominance of Christian men who sought to create a governmental system that would promote justice. These men understood that if our nation ever rejected the biblical worldview upon which it was founded, destruction would inevitably result. How devastated they would be if they could see what has happened in recent years.

Our nation's central founding document, the Constitution, has been manipulated—if not entirely ignored—in the pernicious effort to secularize our nation. As a result, catastrophic changes have been imposed on our citizens. Here are a few poignant examples:

- In a flagrant distortion of the First Amendment, prayer and the Ten Commandments have been abolished from schools.
- In the name of privacy, the Supreme Court legalized the murder of the unborn in *Roe v. Wade*.
- In the name of tolerance, hate crimes legislation impedes the free speech of law-abiding citizens.

Regrettably, these are only a few of the many examples of the legal corruption of our Constitution in recent years.

The dearth of moral values in our governing elite has brought us to the verge of social anarchy. And the people who have changed our laws, standards, and community values apparently have no idea what has caused the deterioration of our youth, our crime-ridden streets, and the ineffectiveness of our system of justice. Their solution to these problems? More costly, increasingly futile government programs!

Whenever you talk about Christians and morally committed citizens coming to the aid of their country to once again take positions of leadership in those fields of influence, the secularizers go ballistic. They attack us in the press and media as though the social and political involvement of God-fearing Americans is the worst thing that could happen to America! They forget, or they were never taught, that Christian involvement in all areas of community life is the background of American heritage.

Secularists' attacks often deter writers from projecting what life in America would be like if we experienced a moral and spiritual revival. You may find, as you read these few pages, that you would love to live in an America with a restored conscience, a country where the churches of the nation set the standards for what is acceptable community behavior . . . a time when morality and legality are virtually synonymous . . . a time when everyone is held accountable for his own behavior and understands that fact . . . a time when our gratitude toward God is seen in our generosity toward and concern for those less fortunate than we.

WHAT IF . . . ?

What if all Christians truly repented of their personal and national sins according to 2 Chronicles 7:14 and God healed our land by sending us the revival we so desperately need?

What if all Christians reached out in love to the mental and moral barbarians of our nation—people who are really victims of the secularists who have deceived them about God and his moral absolutes?

What if, in the power of the Holy Spirit, we lovingly and zealously shared with the empty-hearted victims of our secularist society the gospel of salvation through Jesus Christ, leading millions to receive him?

What if Christians took seriously their individual and church responsibilities, and spiritually and morally "turned the world upside down" (that is, right-side up) as did the first-century Christians?

What if our churches were as full on prayer-meeting nights as they are on Sunday mornings? And what if those prayers were offered for the conscience and soul of our nation?

What if Christians of our nation took seriously the call to holiness—"without which no one will see the Lord" (Heb. 12:14)—cleaning up their moral lives and putting God, the family, the church, their fellowman, and their vocations in proper priority?

What if Christian youth were totally committed in obedience to the Word of God to give honor and respect to their parents and to obey those in authority over them?

What if Christian youth committed themselves to God to live holy lives and to fulfill the Great Commission in their lifetime (see Matt. 28:19-20)?

What if we in the church still took seriously the Great Commission given by our Lord and either went out to the lost world or gave generously of our earthly possessions and treasures to enable others to go for us (see 1 John 3:17)?

What if the 52 percent of the Christians who did not vote in the last election became serious about their citizenship responsibilities and went to the polls to vote into office only those candidates who share their commitment to moral values?

What if even 20 percent of the previously nonvoting Christians became politically involved during this decade, electing God-fearing local and state officials, congressmen, senators, as well as a God-fearing president?

What if public servants worked to restore our God-given, unalienable rights of life for the born and unborn, freedom of religious expression, and protection from injustice, as well as the freedom to pursue our dreams and earn our keep, independent of government intrusion?

What if the godless act of abortion were seen as the cruel, conscienceless, and immoral practice it is and were banned from our nation?

What if pornography, pedophilia, and other perverse practices were once again universally viewed as immoral and consequently outlawed throughout the land?

What if our nation effectively curtailed the $10-billion-a-year pornography business?

What if morally minded legislators took charge of the federally controlled airwaves and established standards of decency for television, radio, and entertainment and refused to license stations and networks that violated that code?

What if video and recording studios were required to produce only music and other forms of entertainment that stayed within the law, banning songs that advocate the murder of police officers, the mutilation of women, and child abuse?

What if parents could afford to send their children to the school of their choice?

What if mothers were free to stay at home to raise their babies?

What if churches of all sorts became serious about educating their children academically, spiritually, and morally—providing a quality education with a biblical base?

What if fathers practiced what the Scripture teaches about being the spiritual head of the family?

What if our morally committed legislators officially recognized that this country was indeed "one nation under God" and led the nation to write that fact into law by adding it to the Constitution?

What if voluntary public prayer of the individual's choosing were welcomed in public schools and those who took offense were free to send their children elsewhere?

What if our federal government got out of the education business and closed down the Federal Department of Education with its anti-American, one world, socialist agenda?

What if our schools cancelled the explicit sex education programs that have fostered an obsession with sex among our youth and chose instead to inspire students to spend more time on academic subjects like reading, writing, arithmetic, as well as others that would help prepare them for a meaningful and noble life?

What if all 755 federal judges were committed to upholding the Constitution, enabling the U.S. to once again enjoy "justice under the law," rather than imposing liberal secularist interpretations that promote injustice?

What if the Supreme Court interpreted the laws as the founding fathers intended, rather than according to current whims and personal preferences?

What if Christians and other morally upright citizens were represented in our government in proportion to their actual numbers in the general population, so that true values—not those of the secularizing elite—guided our nation?

What if the federal government returned much of its decision-making power to the individual states according to constitutional design, thus reducing the federal tax bite dramatically?

What if parents demanded that educators stop rewriting history and instead let the facts speak for themselves?

What if our children were taught the accounts of the awesome influence of Christians and others in the founding and development of this country?

What if *truth* were restored to our nation?

If these things came to pass, the entire world would rejoice in the restoration of America's conscience.

If you are interested in keeping up-to-date with the fast-breaking events from Washington, D.C., that affect the family's traditional values and our religious freedoms, you need to receive the LaHaye's two monthly publications. You can receive three months' complimentary issues as a trial by contacting the following offices:

THE FAMILY VOICE PUBLICATION
Concerned Women for America
370 L'Enfant Promenade, S.W.
Suite 800
Washington, DC 20024
1-800-458-8797
($15 for one year)

THE CAPITOL REPORT
Family Life Ministries
P.O. Box 2700
Washington, DC 20013
(202) 488-0700
($15 for one year)

End Notes

INTRODUCTION

1. William Morley Punshon, quoted in *The Encyclopedia of Religious Quotations,* ed. Frank S. Mead (Old Tappan, N.J.: Revell, 1985), 85.

CHAPTER 1

1. William Katz, *An Album of Nazism* (New York: Franklin Watts, 1979), 36.

2. Katina Johnstone, "A Neglected Child, a Gun, a Death . . . ," *San Diego Union,* 21 December 1993.

3. Dan Coats, "Our Tattered Moral Fabric," *The Washington Times,* 23 November 1992, A17.

4. Ibid.

5. Dick Gregory, quoted in *The New York Public Library Book of 20th-Century American Quotations,* eds. Stephen Donadio et al. (New York: Warner Books, 1992), 173.

6. Matt Neufeld, "Mourning Teen Friend, Man Meets Same Fate: Shooting Occurs Outside NE Funeral," *The Washington Times,* 27 December 1993, A1.

7. Joyce Price, "Crime at the Hands of Children," *The Washington Times,* 29 December 1993, A7.

8. Charles W. Colson, "Kids and Crime: Who's Responsible," *Citizen* (December 20, 1993): 10–11.

9. John D. Hull, "Have We Gone Mad?" *Time* Special Report, 20 December 1993, 31.

10. "Selling Children for Spare Parts," *Family Voice,* October 1993, 28–29.

11. *Beyond Rhetoric: A New American Agenda for Children and Families* (Washington, D.C.: National Commission on Children, 1991), 66.

12. "Violence Is Blamed on Family Breakup," *The Washington Times,* 20 September 1993.

13. William J. Bennett, *The Index of Leading Cultural Indicators* (Wash-

ington, D.C.: Empower America, The Heritage Foundation, Free Congress Foundation, 1993), 9.

14. Joyce Price, "Elders Calls Gay Sex 'Wonderful,' 'Healthy,'" *The Washington Times,* 19 March 1994.

15. Don Feder, "The Dead End of Non-Judgmentalism," *The Washington Times,* 4 January 1994.

16. Ibid.

17. Charles W. Colson, *Against the Night: Living in the New Dark Ages* (Ann Arbor, Mich.: Servant Books, 1989), 44.

18. Ibid., 80.

19. Cheryl Wetzstein, "Lesbians Provoke Parents, 'Recruiting' at Grade School," *The Washington Times,* 28 February 1994.

20. Jerry Seper, "At Urging of Justice, High Court Eases Child-Porn Definition," *The Washington Times,* 2 November 1993.

21. Otto Scott, "Psychiatry Discovers Religion," *Chalcedon Report,* no. 345 (April 1994): 3.

22. "Lake County Scuffle in the Culture War," *The Washington Times,* 18 May 1994.

23. David Barton, *America: To Pray or Not to Pray?* (Aledo, Tex.: WallBuilder Press, 1991), 44.

24. Peter Marshall and David Manuel, *The Light and Glory* (Old Tappan, N.J.: Revell, 1977), 342–343.

25. William F. Buckley Jr., quoted in *20th-Century American Quotations,* 12.

CHAPTER 2
1. Zbigniew Brzezinski, *Out of Control: Global Turmoil on the Eve of the Twenty-First Century* (New York: Charles Scribner's Sons, 1993), 4–5.

2. Charles W. Colson, *Against the Night: Living in the New Dark Ages,* (Ann Arbor, Mich.: Servant Books, 1989), 23.

3. David A. Noebel, "From the President's Desk," *Summit Journal* (October 1993): 4.

4. Brzezinski, *Out of Control,* 4–5.

5. Ibid., 17.

6. Ibid., 18.

7. Steve Dougherty, review of *Come As You Are: The Story of Nirvana,* by Michael Azerrad, *People,* 18 April 1994, 36.

8. James Thompson, "Walker Percy's Guide for the Perplexed," *The World & I,* January 1994, 413.

9. Brzezinski, *Out of Control,* 10.

10. Stanley K. Henshaw, "Induced Abortion: A World Review, 1990," *Family Planning Perspectives* 22, no. 2, (March/ April 1990): 76.

11. *Congressional Record,* 1993, 4322.

12. Thompson, "Walker Percy's Guide," 413.

13. Russell Kirk, *America's British Culture* (New Brunswick, N.J.: Transaction Publishers, 1993), 90.

14. Francis A. Schaeffer, *How Should We Then Live: The Rise and Decline of Western Thought and Culture* (Old Tappan, N.J.: Revell, 1976), 227.

15. Ibid., 205.

16. *TV: The World's Greatest Mind-Bender* (New York: Morality in Media, 1993), 7.

17. R. C. Sproul, *Lifeviews: Understanding the Ideas That Shape Society Today* (Old Tappan, N.J.: Revell, 1980), 136–37.

18. "Art on the Cutting Edge," *Newsweek,* 11 April 1994, 79.

19. Jo Ann Lewis, "What's Art? (What's Not?)" *The Washington Post,* 24 October 1993.

20. Ibid.

21. Patrick Buchanan, "Drawing a Line in the Cultural Combat Zone," *The Washington Times,* 11 September 1992.

22. Aleksandr Solzhenitsyn, "How the Cult of Novelty Wrecked the 20th Century," *American Arts Quarterly* (spring 1993): 18.

23. Ibid.

24. Ibid.

25. Ibid., 20.

26. Robert Nisbet, "Still Questing," *Intercollegiate Review* 29, no. 1 (fall 1993): 43.

27. Senator Carter Glass, Democrat of Virginia, Ashland, Virginia, July 19, 1936, as quoted in *Quotations from Addresses, Messages and Statements about the New Deal by New Dealers and Democrats* (Republican National Committee).

28. Joseph Sobran, "The Autocracy of Rights," *The Washington Times,* 9 December 1993.

29. Thomas Sowell, "History All on the Side of Jefferson," *The Washington Times,* 29 April 1993.

30. William Buckley Jr., "Public Service and the Lure of Power," *The Washington Times,* 1 February 1993.

31. John W. Wimberly Jr., "Feeding the Homeless—A Matter of Religious Liberty," *The Washington Post,* 8 March 1994.

32. Joe Mathews, "Beavis, Butt-Head & Budding Nihilists: Will Western Civilization Survive?" *The Washington Post,* 3 October 1993.

33. Colson, *Against the Night,* 13.

CHAPTER 3
1. David Barton, *America: To Pray or Not to Pray?* (Aledo, Tex.: Wallbuilder Press, 1991), 89.

2. Benjamin Franklin, quoted in *The Encyclopedia of Religious Quotations,* ed. Frank S. Mead (Old Tappan, N.J.: Revell, 1985), 84.

3. Barton, *America,* 109.

4. Ibid., 110.

5. Benjamin Franklin, "Advice on Coming to America," *America in Person,* ed. George D. Youstra (Greenville, S.C.: Bob Jones University Press, 1975), 109.

6. Francis A. Schaeffer, *A Christian Manifesto* (Wheaton, Ill.: Crossway, 1982), 31–32.

7. Gaillard Hunt, *James Madison and Religious Liberty* (Washington, D.C.: American Historical Association, Government Printing Office, 1902), 66.

8. From an unabridged, printed sermon by D. James Kennedy, "Church and State," used by permission.

9. *Journals of the Continental Congress, 1774–1789* (Washington, D.C.: Government Printing Office, 1907), 8:731–35.

10. Alexis de Tocqueville, *Democracy in America,* Volume I (New York: Vintage Books, 1945), 23, 314–15, 319.

11. Barton, *America,* 9.

12. Dwight D. Eisenhower, quoted in *The New York Public Library Book of 20th-Century American Quotations,* ed. Stephen Donadio, et al. (New York: Warner Books, 1992), 13.

13. John Frederick Schroeder, ed., *Maxims of Washington* (New York: D. Appleton, 1855), 311.

14. Russell Kirk, ed., *The Assault on Religion: Commentaries on the Decline of Religious Liberty* (New York: University Press of America, 1986), 4.

15. Larry Burkett, *What Ever Happened to the American Dream?* (Chicago: Moody Press, 1993), 29.

16. Bruce Fein, "Criminal Cop-Outs with Benchmarks," *The Washington Times,* 20 October 1993.

17. Ibid.

18. Burkett, *American Dream,* 29.

19. David G. Savage, "School Prayer Is Born Again in Texas Town's High School," *Tampa Tribune,* 17 April 1994, A-14.

20. Josiah Royce, quoted in *20th-Century American Quotations,* 174.

CHAPTER 4
1. Charles Buxton, quoted in *The Encyclopedia of Religious Quotations,* ed. Frank S. Mead (Old Tappan, N.J.: Revell, 1985), 84.

2. James Russell Lowell, quoted in *Encyclopedia of Religious Quotations,* 85.

3. Wirthlin Group, telephone survey of 1,000 adults, June 17–19, 1991.

4. William J. Bennett, *The Index of Leading Cultural Indicators* (Washington, D.C.: Empower America, The Heritage Foundation, Free Congress Foundation, 1993), 17.

5. R. C. Sproul, "A Two-Handed King: Church and State Are Separate, but Also under God," *World,* 22 January 1994, 26.

6. Karen S. Peterson, "Poll: 59 Percent Call Religion Important," *USA Today,* 13 April 1994.

CHAPTER 5
1. William M. Welch, "Age-Old Debate on Morality Takes New Life," *USA Today,* 15 December 1993.

2. Remarks by Vice President Quayle to the Commonwealth Club of California (San Francisco, Calif.), May 19, 1992.

3. Michael Medved, *Hollywood vs. America: Popular Culture and the War on Traditional Values* (New York: HarperCollins Publishers, Inc., 1992), 48.

4. Barbara Dafoe Whitehead, "Dan Quayle Was Right," *Atlantic Monthly,* April 1993, 84.

5. Ibid.

6. Joyce Price, "Crime at the Hands of Children," *The Washington Times,* 29 December 1993.

7. Ibid.

8. Dr. Ken Magid and Carole A. McKelvey, *High Risk: Children without a Conscience* (New York: Bantam Books, 1988), 110, 119.

9. Welch, "Age-Old Debate on Morality."

10. Beverly LaHaye, *The Desires of a Woman's Heart* (Wheaton, Ill.: Tyndale House, 1993), 187–88.

11. Barbara Vobejda, "6 Million of Nation's Youngest Children Face Developmental Risks," *The Washington Post,* 13 April 1994, A3.

12. Nanci Hellmich, "Children at Risk: A 'Quiet Crisis,'" *USA Today,* 13 April 1994, 4D.

13. Associated Press, "Massachusetts City Recognizes Gay Couples," *The Washington Times,* 17 November 1992.

14. *Lambda Report* I, no. 5, October 1993, 7.

15. Fran Sciacca, *Generation at Risk: What Legacy Are the Baby-Boomers Leaving Their Kids?* (Chicago: Moody Press, 1990), 141.

16. LaHaye, *Desires*, 20.

17. Bryce J. Christensen, "America's 'Retreat from Marriage,'" *The Family in America* 2, no. 2 (February 1988): 8.

CHAPTER 6

1. John Bartlett, *Bartlett's Familiar Quotations* (Boston: Little, Brown and Company, 1982), 777.

2. E. C. McKenzie, *14,000 Quips & Quotes* (New York: Wings Books, 1980), 105.

3. Lord Acton, quoted in *Bartlett's Familiar Quotations*, 615.

4. Catherine Boehme, "Euthanasia: What Is Your Net Worth?" *Charter Oak* (February/March 1994).

5. Barry M. Goldwater, quoted in *The New York Public Library Book of 20th-Century American Quotations*, ed. Stephen Donadio, et al. (New York: Warner Books, 1992), 364.

6. Lawrence Criner, "Waco: The Tragic Collision of Religious and Secular Mind-sets," *The Washington Times*, 4 March 1994.

7. John F. Kennedy, quoted in *20th-Century American Quotations*, 364.

8. Francois Rabelais, quoted in *Bartlett's Familiar Quotations*, 157.

9. Samuel L. Blumenfeld, *Is Public Education Necessary?* (Boise, Idaho: Paradigm Co., 1985), 105.

10. Ibid., 118.

11. Bill Belz, "Pagan People Can't Think: Even When They Reach Right Conclusions, They're Mixed Up," *World*, 22 January 1994, 3.

12. Kathleen M. Gow, *Yes, Virginia, There Is Right and Wrong* (Wheaton, Ill.: Tyndale House, 1985), 174.

CHAPTER 7

1. John T. McNicholas, quoted in *The New York Public Library Book of 20th-Century American Quotations*, ed. Stephen Donadio, et al. (New York: Warner Books, 1992), 365.

2. William Jennings Bryan, quoted in *20th-Century American Quotations*, 364.

3. Don Feder, "'Omm' Echoes from Harvard," *The Washington Times*, 4 March 1994.

4. Ibid.

5. Ibid.

6. Ibid.

7. William Benton, *The Annals of America*, vol. 3 (Chicago: Encyclopedia Britannica, 1968), 194–95.

8. John C. Fitzpatrick, ed., *The Writings of George Washington*, vol. 35 (Washington, D.C.: Government Printing Office, 1940), 229.

9. McDowell and Beliles, *America's Providential History* (San Diego: Providence Press, 1988), 163.

10. Robert Flood, *The Rebirth of America* (Philadelphia: The Arthur DeMoss Foundation, 1986), 33.

11. David Barton, *The Myth of Separation: What is the Correct Relationship between Church and State?* (Aledo, Tex.: WallBuilder Press, 1989), 125.

12. Ibid., 124–25.

13. *World Book Encyclopedia*, vol. 17 (Chicago: World Book, Inc., 1993), 317.

14. Samuel L. Blumenfeld, *Is Public Education Necessary?* (Boise, Idaho: Paradigm Co., 1985), 27.

15. Ibid., 28.

16. Ibid., 30.

17. Ibid., 95–96.

18. Ibid., 43.

19. Tribune Wire Report, "Creationism Costs Job," *Tampa Tribune*, 13 April 1994, A2.

20. Blumenfeld, *Public Education*, 166.

21. Ibid., 165.

22. Ibid., 192,

23. Ibid., 247.

CHAPTER 8

1. John Milton, quoted in *The Encyclopedia of Religious Quotations,* ed. Frank S. Mead (Old Tappan, N.J.: Revell, 1985), 85.

2. S. Robert Lichter and Stanley Rothman, "Media & Business Elites," *Public Opinion,* October/November 1981, 42.

3. Stephen Strang, "The Power Within," *Charisma,* January 1983.

4. "Watt Lauds His Tenure, Assails Media for Distortion," *San Diego Union,* 8 February 1983, A-3.

5. James Reston, *The Artillery of the Press* (New York: Harper & Row, 1967), vii.

6. Leonard Silk and Mark Silf, *The American Establishment* (New York: Basic Books, 1980), 68.

7. Theodore Baehr, *Getting the Word Out* (San Francisco: Harper & Row, 1986), 117.

8. L. Brent Bozell III, "Delayed Reflections in the Looking Glass," *The Washington Times,* 22 March 1994, A-24.

9. Ibid.

10. Maureen Dowd, "Hillary Rodham Clinton Strikes a New Pose and Multiplies Her Images," *New York Times,* 12 December 1993.

11. Barry Golson and Peter Ross Range, "Clinton on TV," *TV Guide,* 21 November 1992, 15.

12. Ibid., 14.

13. Ibid.

14. Patrick J. Buchanan, "Big Media Go Easy on Clinton," *San Francisco Examiner,* 15 March 1994.

15. Michael Medved, *Hollywood v. America: Popular Culture and the War on Traditional Values* (New York: HarperCollins Publishers, Inc., 1992), 344–45.

16. *TV: The World's Greatest Mind-Bender* (New York: Morality in Media, 1993), 7–8.

17. Baehr, *Getting the Word Out,* 116.

18. Ibid., 117.

19. Madonna, quoted in *The Advocate,* 21 May 1991, 40.

20. Angela Elwell Hunt, "Ted Baehr: Taking Every Thought Captive," *Fundamentalist Journal*, June 1989, 52.

21. *Movieguide* is a Christian newsletter for parents who seek biblically based reviews of current movies so they can make wise choices for themselves and their children. For a one-year subscription, send $40 to MOVIEGUIDE, Good News Communications, P.O. Box 190010, Atlanta, GA 31119.

22. Medved, *Hollywood v. America,* 58.

23. Ibid., 45–49.

24. Ibid., 67–68.

25. E. C. McKenzie, *14,000 Quips & Quotes* (New York: Wings Books, 1980), 105.

CHAPTER 9

1. Henry Clay Trumbull, quoted in *The Encyclopedia of Religious Quotations*, ed. Frank S. Mead (Old Tappan, N.J.: Revell, 1985), 86.

2. Larry P. Arnn and Douglas A. Jeffrey, eds., *Moral Ideas for America* (Claremont, Calif.: The Claremont Institute, 1993), 37.

3. Marlise Simons, "Dutch Parliament Approves Law Permitting Euthanasia," *New York Times International,* 10 February 1993.

4. "Euthanasia Practice in Holland," *International Anti-Euthanasia Task Force Fact Sheet* (December 1993).

5. George Barna, *The Frog in the Kettle: What Christians Need to Know About Life in the Year 2000* (Ventura, Calif.: Regal Books, 1990), 112–13.

6. Ted Baehr, *The Movie & Video Guide for Christian Families* (Nashville, Tenn.: Nelson, 1987), 18.

7. Les Brown, *Keeping Your Eye on Television* (New York: Pilgrim Press, 1979), 8.

8. "Unilever number one sponsor of TV filth," *American Family Association Journal* (April 1994): 1.

9. Tom McNichol, "The New Sex Vow: 'I Won't Until I Do,'" *Sunday Times,* 25–7 March 1994.

CHAPTER 10

1. John F. MacArthur Jr., *The Vanishing Conscience: Drawing the Line in a No-Fault, Guilt-Free World* (Irving, Tex.: Word, 1994), 12.

2. Erwin W. Lutzer, *Why Are We the Enemy?* (Chicago: Moody Press, 1993), 21–22.

3. Martin Luther King Jr., quoted in *The New York Public Library Book of 20th-Century American Quotations,* ed. Stephen Donadio, et al. (New York: Warner Books, 1992), 365.

4. Francis A. Schaeffer, *A Christian Manifesto* (Wheaton, Ill.: Crossway, 1981), 45.

A Nation without a Conscience is also available on Tyndale Living
Audio. 0-8423-7432-9

Also by Beverly LaHaye

THE DESIRES OF A WOMAN'S HEART 0-8423-1372-9
Encouragement for women to pursue traditional Christian values of
home and family, personal fulfillment, and a relationship with God.

Additional titles from Tim LaHaye

THE BEGINNING OF THE END 0-8423-0264-6
Recently revised, this scripturally based book directs believers to
prepare for Christ's second coming.

HOW TO BE HAPPY THOUGH MARRIED 0-8423-1499-7
Best-selling advice on developing physical, mental, and spiritual
harmony in marriage.

SPIRIT-CONTROLLED TEMPERAMENT 0-8423-6220-7
A superb treatment of the four basic human temperaments and their
spiritual potential, now with new chapters and discussion questions.

TRANSFORMED TEMPERAMENTS 0-8423-7304-7
Discover God's transforming power through this character analysis of
Abraham, Moses, Peter, and Paul.

**WHAT EVERYONE SHOULD KNOW ABOUT
HOMOSEXUALITY** 0-8423-7933-9
This critical look at the homosexual explosion offers significant
insights for concerned readers.

WHY YOU ACT THE WAY YOU DO 0-8423-8212-7
Learn how your temperament affects your work, emotions,
relationships, and spiritual life as well as how to make improvements.